T0067491

# DON'T FEAR DEATH!

MICHAEL WORT

BALBOA.PRESS
A DIVISION OF HAY HOUSE

Balboa Press books may be ordered through booksellers or by contacting:

Balboa Press
A Division of Hay House
1663 Liberty Drive
Bloomington, IN 47403
www.balboapress.com.au
AU TFN: 1 800 844 925 (Toll Free inside Australia)
AU Local: 0283 107 086 (+61 2 8310 7086 from outside Australia)



Print information available on the last page.

ISBN: 978-1-5043-2461-8 (sc)
ISBN: 978-1-5043-2462-5 (e)

Balboa Press rev. date: 02/15/2021

# CONTENTS

# PREFACE

I always consider myself lucky to have had a very interesting life, having visited many countries and experienced many different cultures, some albeit only briefly.

My enthusiasm for life remains undiminished, and is part of the reasons for why I have written this book. I have always believed that life has a purpose, that we are not here for no specific reason. Very definitely we are not here 'by chance'.

It always dismays me to meet people who think the opposite. An all too common attitude is "Life sucks, and then you die."

As a scientifically trained person, with a university degree already under my belt, in my early adult life I did my best not to think about the end-game, about the inevitability of death. When I used to drive to my university in London for post-grad studies, there was a point on the South Circular road which runs around south London near the St Dunstan's College school where an old grey church stood, with stone-work blackened by many years of exposure to the London air. For some reason, seeing this church as I drove to and from college always reminded me of this inevitability.

Much later in life, approaching my forties, I began to take a greater interest in the reasons for why we are all here, and started reading about religions other than Christianity including Buddhism and the Hindu religion. I also joined the Rosicrucians, a mystical group with teachings about things like clairvoyance and occult philosophies like the Kabbala. Then in 1994 I joined a group following the teachings of Sri Sathya Sai Baba, an Indian spiritual teacher, who taught that all the major religions are basically good. Sai Baba's teachings and the experiences I have had both in Australia and at his ashram at Puttaparthi in India have completely changed my attitude, removed my fear of death, and given me an unshakeable belief in the loving presence of God.

As Sai Baba has said, life is a challenge! The purpose of our life is to rise and meet that challenge!

# INTRODUCTION

The following account is the true story of my life from my earliest memories as a small child living in the south of England, up to the present in January 2021.

While the names of some of the people featuring in my account have been changed, the incidents themselves are true events.

Along with the chapters covering specific stages in my life, I have placed other chapters presenting some of my experiences and insights collected along the way.

# 1

# THE SAGA BEGINS

The Garmoyle Nursing Home was a pleasant looking building on the north side of a road in the little seaside town of Shanklin, Isle of Wight. It was here, at 3 a.m. on the morning of September 12$^{th}$, 1942, that I came into this world.

My earliest memories of family members other than my mother Joan, included my maternal grandmother Ethel, and my grandfather Jimmy. Grampa was a Methodist minister, and I was christened in the little Methodist church in Shanklin village. Joan was the eldest of five children, and I quickly came to know her siblings Keith, Gwen, Betty and Russell. Russell, the youngest, would be off to Cambridge soon to study medicine after completing his schooldays at Kingswood, and he quickly became my favourite uncle. It was he who took me for my first swim off Shanklin beach, sitting on his back and hanging grimly round his neck while he swam around leisurely in the calm waters close to shore. It was also he who would give me shoulder rides as we walked along the path which ran north to Sandown along the steep cliffs.

Of course, I saw a lot of Granma and Grampa. They lived in a great big two-storey house at the end of Howard Road in Shanklin, close to the cliffs. The garden was large, and flanked on one side by some huge pine trees, whose cones I loved to collect. On the other side, the house was flanked by some tennis courts. I became very fond of their two lovely golden Cocker Spaniel dogs, Tess and Pedro, and fondly remember walks along the cliffs with them.

Sadly, my earliest memories do not include my father, Ernest. He was away in India and Burma when I was born, having joined the Territorials before the war started, and was then posted to fight the Japanese. He had joined up after a holiday to Austria, where he had seen German munitions factories working all day and through the night. It became clear to him that the Germans were preparing for war. His patriotic sacrifice meant that he did not follow in his father's footsteps as the owner of the Littlehampton Electricity Company. In later years he continued to keep in touch with some old family friends in Littlehampton, Mr & Mrs Illman.

My memory of my grandparents on my father's side is almost non-existent. I only recall a wooden rocking horse that was made for me by Ernest's father, Arthur Lewis Wort. The imprint of his name is still on the haft of some of his tools which were left to me by my father. Ernest's parents were killed during the war, when their house in south-east London in the suburb of Lee received a direct hit from a German bomb.

My own memories of the war are limited to the sound of bombers flying over head, as I lay in my little bed at 10 Eastcliff Road, Shanklin. It was here that I lived with my mother during those war years, and the home to which my father returned in 1945 when I was three years old. The front garden was less than pocket-handkerchief sized, and the only thing that grew in it were some dark red wallflowers. The back garden was bigger, but at a much higher level than the ground floor of the house, and had to be reached by climbing a steep wooden staircase.

My mother told me when I was older that one day, while she was pushing me in my pram along the Shanklin cliffs, she had to duck as a German fighter plane roared low over the cliff tops with a British fighter right behind, guns blazing. The German plane crashed into the sea close to the end of Shanklin pier.

My father was a sergeant in the Royal Signals and in India became a lieutenant and was posted with his men to Northern Burma. With his signals team he was on a hilltop position to ensure good radio communications. The Japanese invasion of Burma had begun, and more and more Japanese fighter planes were seen by my father and his team. A few days went by, and my father sent an orderly down to check with the regiment in the main camp, from whom they had not heard for a few days. The orderly returned with grim news - the regiment had decamped for retreat to India, with no warning given to the signals group! My father and his men immediately broke camp and managed to get back into Assam by the skin of their teeth.

When my father came home from the war I remember that we used to have our meals in the front room on the ground floor. For breakfast it was usually porridge with milk and sugar. I had a special teaspoon with a curled up handle, that I could hold by sticking my thumb through the loop. One day I let go of it, and it disappeared into the porridge, about the first time that I can remember crying.

I used to play with a tin fort and some lead soldiers. One day I got mad with the fort and jumped on it repeatedly and reduced it to flat metal, my first lesson of why it is not a good idea to lose one's temper!

In due course my father was offered back his pre-war job in Greenwich on the Thames, and he went off to London to find us some accommodation. Once he had done this we left Shanklin to join him.

# 2

# Post-war London

In 1947 when I was about five we moved as a family to London. My father had gone ahead in advance, to continue working for the company he had joined before the war - Siemens AEI. They took him back on the same pay into the same position he had had before he left to join the war. His job was as a telecommunications engineer, and he shortly became a Group Leader, managing a team that was working on the design of telephone exchanges mainly for export to overseas countries like Australia and South Africa. He drew heavily on the training he had acquired as an officer in the Royal Signals, the regiment he had fought with in Burma against the Japanese.

He had picked out a ground floor flat at 29 St Mildred's Road in Lee, a south-east London suburb. The house was on the corner with Birch Grove, diagonally opposite St Mildred's Church. We were also just up the road from the house in Newstead Road that my father's parents had lived in, still in ruins from the time that they were both killed by a direct hit from a German bomb.

We lived on the ground floor and the upstairs flat was occupied by an old lady, Mrs Salmon, and her son Roy, who was a policeman and altogether more friendly and less cantankerous.

Being after the war, the British public was on food rationing, so that we could send food to our former enemies, the Germans. Fresh eggs were unobtainable, and my mother made omelettes from a tin of powdered egg yolk. Very rarely we were able to obtain some real eggs from a farmer friend on the Isle of Wight. Chocolates and sugar were only obtainable with coupons. Occasionally my father's army friend, John Avis, would bring us a pheasant that he had accidently killed while driving to see us from Bury St Edmunds in Suffolk, where he lived. John was also my Godfather, and would always bring me a treat.

I started at the local primary School, Manor Lane, which involved a lengthy walk. My first teacher was Mrs Smith, a dark-haired lady. I did not really enjoy Manor Lane, and got into trouble several times, once for continuing to play football after the end-of-break whistle had blown. However, Manor Lane did have one redeeming feature. Just down the road, in the middle of a section of terraced houses which ran down to Hither Green, lived Aunt Ciss and Uncle Walter, and from time to time in the summer they would invite me for tea, usually a lovely salad of sliced ham, new potatoes cooked with mint, plus some lettuce and tomatoes. Walter had a business making high quality children's clothes, and Ciss helped him by doing the book-keeping and accounts. Walter's birthday was on March 26th, the same day as for my father and also my Godfather, John Avis. Walter was a solidly built man, and I remember his jovial manner and thick, square framed glasses. Above all he loved a feed of crab. Sometimes in the summer my parents, Walter, Ciss and I would all go to a place on farmland near Westerham in Kent, where we would enjoy a lovely picnic under the trees while taking care to avoid the cow pats that were liberally sprinkled over the field.

The garden at No. 29 was rather scruffy, but pleasant enough. I remember a pear tree which I loved to climb, and the little second-hand tricycle which my father got for me and which I would ride around the garden, and down the adjoining pavement of Birch Grove when I could. The front garden had some buddleia bushes on whose flowers the butterflies would feast in summer. I remember happy hours chasing butterflies. Red Admirals, Peacocks, Tortoiseshells, and the occasional and stunning Camberwell Beauty and of course the endless Cabbage Whites which true to their name would lay their eggs on my father's cabbages in the back garden. The front garden also had a privet hedge down one side, the food source for a brightly striped black and yellow caterpillar of a common moth. My butterfly collection grew, and I would practice setting their wings on some cork setting boards given to me by Aunt Gwen and Uncle Harry, who lived at Newport on the Isle of Wight, just down the road from the historically famous Carisbrooke Castle. Earlier, as a small boy, I had attended Gwen and Harry's wedding, the first that I can remember. I was bought a new little brown suit to wear for the occasion. Later they had two sons - my cousins Russell and Simon. I spent many happy summers at their Newport house, and became a frequent visitor to the castle, which had served as a prison for King Charles 1st before he was taken to London for execution by the Roundheads. The castle also had an exciting well, for which the bucket was raised and lowered by a friendly old donkey who walked up and down a tread-wheel. Harry had a passion for water-colour painting, at which he was exceedingly good. He had also done a remarkable copy of the famous "Laughing Cavalier" oil painting. I used to spend hours reading through his copies of National Geographic, or being entranced by stories about the American frontier in the famous "Boy's Own Paper".

It must have been around 1952 when we moved to a new house in a distant part of Lee, at 113 Guibal Road. This was close to Grove Park and Eltham, both of which lay in Kent. Our bedrooms were upstairs and mine was at the back, from where I had a stunning view towards Eltham and the famous Shot Tower. This was the start of a new and happy period in my life. The house was newly constructed on the remains of a house destroyed by bombing during the war. The garden was completely overgrown with wild blackberry bushes and bracken, with tall grass. Partridges were still nesting there, and hedgehogs were regular tenants. There was even a semi-tame grey rabbit, which I think had escaped from a hutch somewhere. In the right-hand corner of the back garden was a tall poplar tree, which

I loved to climb, even though it was really in the garden of our neighbours, Reg and Cathy Wright. Across the width of the back, and abutting a barren strip of ground which lay beyond, were four nice apple trees. In the left hand corner, on the waste strip, was a weeping ash. Beneath this I built a little cubby house.

Down the hill about a mile from our house was a shallow valley with some woods and a little stream, the Quaggy River. Beyond the Quaggy was some open farmland. The Quaggy carried little fish called sticklebacks, also some minnows. In summer the sticklebacks were breeding and the males would get a red belly. I used to go fishing for them with a little net on the end of a short bamboo stick, and would carry them home in a jam jar to place in our aquarium, where I also used to keep baby frogs and occasionally also newts.

It took us a long time to clear the scrub away from our back garden, but eventually my father had laid some concrete paths and we had a vegetable and fruit garden at the bottom, a lawn grown from laid turf in the middle, and a pleasant rockery close to the house, which was set above the rockery. My father also laid a concrete base, and erected an asbestos sheeting shed - in those days the perils of asbestos had not been realised. It was here in the Guibal Road garden that I got my first lessons in digging, lawn mowing, rose pruning, fruit picking and storing, and other useful things which I would come to use again many years later. I remember feasting on the black currants, red currants, gooseberries and strawberries which my father grew. In those days our milk was delivered by a horse-drawn cart. The horse obligingly left his droppings around the milkman's round, and I used to go out and collect them with a little shovel in an old sack, and once even gave my father a bag full for his birthday present! He appreciated my gift as he knew how many streets I must have combed to collect it, and applied it lovingly to his roses and the strawberries.

The new house also meant that I had to go to a new school, and I commenced at the Burnt Ash Lane primary school, a shabby and tiny affair with flimsy buildings and a tiny playground. My teacher,

Miss Pickford, had a flair for painting and showed us some lovely paintings of idyllic tropical beaches complete with white sand, blue water and fringing coconut palms. I had developed an early liking for poetry, and was silly enough to make this known to her. For my pains I was made to recite the verses of Christopher Marlowe's poem on "The Passionate Shepherd to His Love", a poem all the more meaningful because I had developed a crush for Adele Carr, a lovely dark haired girl who lived across the road from us at the huge No.95. I would regularly play with Adele and her elder sister Lorraine, and her younger brother Lance. Their father had come from South Africa, and had a big car which was the envy of my poor father who could not afford one. In the playground I handed Adele my first love letter, and was miffed when she promptly complained to her teacher.

Our winter heating was provided by an open coal fire in our living room, and the coal came in sacks that were emptied into a built-in coal shed at one side of the rockery.

I think it was my Uncle Russell who introduced me to bird watching, and the garden at 113 Guibal was a great place for it. In the hawthorn hedge on one side we would have nesting hedge sparrows and long-tailed tits, also chaffinches. House sparrows lived up in the eaves and would chirp all day from sunrise to sunset. In summer we would have migrant swifts that also nested up in the eaves and would play follow my leader in a squealing erratic procession as they flew fast between us and our neighbours' house.

While we were digging in the garden, there would always be a friendly robin perched nearby, who would flit down to grab a tasty worm that we had turned up while digging, and would serenade us with his cheerful song. In the mornings we would listen to the male blackbirds singing their heart out, with song thrushes also chiming in over the top. In winter when the apple trees were essentially bare of leaves, we were visited by a large green parrot, an escapee from an aviary, which survived by eating the withered apples left near the top of our fruit trees.

I forget exactly when, but I was about eleven years old when my parents decided that I would benefit from private schooling. So I then found myself with a very long walk indeed, to a little school slightly beyond the position of our old house, in Newstead Road, close to our old residence at St Mildred's. The matron was a big no-nonsense woman, Mrs Massey. The school, Hamilton House, had a uniform, and I had to wear a blazer and a little cap with dark green stripes. I found myself in the class of Miss Heywood, a formidable old lady with curly hair and a flat hat jammed down upon it, with a craggy face a little bit like Grandma's in the famous Giles cartoons. She always looked at me with a "look what the cat's brought in" expression on her face. In this class I met my next crush, another brunette called Barbara. But Barbara was not all that interested, although I did ride round to her house one day on my new two-wheeler touring bike, a handsome New Yorker painted in red and white enamel with white-walled tyres. The bike was a good one, and was to last me all through my secondary school days.

One day my father brought a visitor from his company home to have dinner with us. His name was Mr Cruttenden. He told us tales of the aboriginal people in Australia, and how they hunted the wild life using their boomerangs. I remember him telling us how they would cook an echidna, the Australian version of a hedgehog, with a back and sides covered with long sharp spines. The aborigines would encase them in a ball of clay, then cook them in hot coals and ashes raked up from a fire. When cooked they would crack the now hard ball of clay open, and eat the tender meat inside.

Around this time my father was offered the opportunity for us to transfer as a family to Australia. Being a very careful man, he thoroughly investigated the price of everything in Australia, like milk, meat, potatoes and other vegetables, newspapers and petrol.

He calculated that on the salary he was offered, that we as a family would be worse off, so he declined the offer. Later one of his colleagues accepted the offer, and I acquired a lot of interesting books owned by their son that they could not take with them.

The dreaded 11-plus exam came and went. By this time I had progressed to Miss Anderson's class. Miss Anderson was tall and slender, a strict woman but a good teacher. I was beginning to excel at English, and at any rate was offered a scholarship by London County Council on the basis of my 11-plus result. (The examiner must have liked my essay, which was entitled "A day in the life of a mouse"). My mother bought me a pair of binoculars as a reward for doing well. It seemed the LCC had a boarding school, which had previously been a tough-as-nails training college for merchant seamen. The good news was that it was far from London, in the beautiful Suffolk countryside adjoining the River Orwell which flowed out to the east coast from Ipswich. There were fees of course, but they were means tested. Nevertheless, I believe it involved considerable sacrifice from my parents to send me there. But they did, and I will always be grateful to them for that.

# 3

# Boarding School in the English Countryside

I was 12 years old when I arrived at Woolverstone Hall for the first time at the beginning of October 1954. Situated about sixteen miles outside Ipswich in the beautiful Suffolk countryside, the school lay on the south bank of the tidal river Orwell, close to the picturesque village of Pin Mill.

The main building of the school was a spectacular Georgian mansion, laying some distance off the main Shotley-Ipswich road, and approached via a long drive lined with trees, which wound past the old Woolverstone church with its square tower reputedly dating back to the 12$^{th}$ century. Other buildings had been erected in the grounds around, including quite a few round-roofed Nissen huts, a legacy of the nautical training school. Some of the Nissen huts were still in use as dormitories for the junior pupils, while others were in use as classrooms. There were other more modern dormitory buildings too, and a large gymnasium over near where the teachers lived in buildings which had previously housed the servants, and grooms for the horses in the stables. Modern classrooms for physics and a large assembly hall had been built closer to the main building which had a large central courtyard with a circular drive, flanked by imposing wings on the left and right. The grounds were extensive and included space for rugby fields and cricket pitches. On the river side there were spectacular views across the Orwell, and the grounds sloped down through a belt of woodland to the river bank and the saltings, composed of salt resistant grass with many muddy patches and pools, that used to get waterlogged at high tide. The woodland belt included the headmaster's garden, a beautifully landscaped area of open grass interspersed with trees and thick bushes of rhododendrons and bamboo thickets, with several narrow paths. The bushes and thickets provided a wonderful nesting area for many species of birds, and it was here that I was later to do much of my birdwatching.

But first there was the important business of settling in and meeting the older boys. Myself and the other "newgies" were good sport, and provided a convenient target for arm pummelling and abuse. Fortunately, the nautical school practice of initiating new boys by removing their trousers and dragging them bare-bottomed through the thick beds of stinging nettles that occurred in the woodland belt had been outlawed by the then school management. There was also the important business of adjusting to your peer-group and the inevitable squabbles and fisticuffs until the pecking order had been sorted out and things settled down into a seeming normality.

I was horribly homesick at first, and hated my Nissen hut dormitory, and the prefect who would come down the aisle along the line of our beds, pummelling anyone who he thought had dared to squeak after lights out. Then there was the footrot, a fungal infection that eats the skin between the toes, an affliction which I have periodically to this day. We all had to shower in an old toilet block, barefoot upon a concrete floor. Soon the whole school had footrot, and we all had to walk ceremoniously both on the way into the shower area and again on our way back out, through a tray filled with red-pink potassium permanganate solution. Our feet took on a perpetual purplish tint. But the horrors of school only lasted three months or so, and then we would all get on a big coach for the 80-odd mile trip back to London for the school holidays. In an amazingly short time I settled in, and fending for myself undoubtedly was good training. I never had many friends, being something of a loner, but of course had a few good buddies.

One of my good friends was an older boy, Dave Harris, who coached me in bird watching, and how to put coloured plastic rings on nestlings' legs. The parkland and wooded belts around the school were rich in birdlife. In winter we had many species of ducks and waders that frequented the Orwell shoreline and saltings. In summer we had a wonderful selection of migrants that stayed to nest - blackcaps and whitethroats, flycatchers, willow warblers, swallows, swifts and house martins etc. The resident birds were lovely too - treecreepers and nuthatches, green woodpeckers and the occasional pied woodpecker, yellowhammers, barn owls, raucous jackdaws and the occasional rook colony, and so on. The jackdaws were actually the biggest problem, as they would regularly take eggs and nestlings from the nests I was observing, sometimes just killing the birds and not even eating them. Resident waders included redshank and curlew, with lapwings also nesting. In late autumn we had visiting European thrushes, the fieldfares and redwings, and occasionally, colourful waxwings too. In winter we had knot and dunlin, and even sanderling down on the saltings.

I came to know every inch of the Orwell bank, for miles on each side of the school. One of the highlights of my schoolboy bird watching was to find a shellduck's nest, inside but close to the edge of a big bramble patch, complete with eggs, and hold an egg as it was hatching. With hindsight I now know that this was not a good thing to do, as ducks and geese identify the first being that they set eyes on as their mother!

No-one played soccer at Woolverstone. Ours was a rugby-playing school. The rugby coach was Taffy Evans, a Welshman to the core. He was also the House-Master of Hall's House, the residential house to which I belonged. The original Mr Hall had left, but the other three houses still had their original incumbents in charge, namely Mr Hanson, Mr Corner, and Mr Johnson. As far as rugger was concerned, Taffy coached us well, and the Woolverstone First Fifteen was a force to be reckoned with! Other prestigious schools in the area were played, including Ipswich Grammar School, Shotley Naval College, Colchester, and some distant public schools whose names I can't now remember. I never made it into the First Fifteen, but played regularly for the Second Fifteen.

Our other winter-time sporting activity was cross-country running. There was a two and a half mile circuit that went from the school down the Cathouse road to the hard and onto the foreshore, then along the edge of the saltings to Pinmill, then back through tiny lanes and across a few fields to the school. Regularly on the day of the inter-house cross country, we would be provided with an unusually good lunch, and I would stuff myself with cauliflower cheese or whatever the dish was, only to regurgitate it along the way during the race, often with terrible accompanying stomach cramps. It was only later, as my schooldays were drawing to a close, that I learnt the wisdom of eating only very lightly, and with minimal or no cramps, performed much better. My best effort was to come 14$^{th}$ in a field where the winner crossed the tape in about 12 and a half minutes. On another occasion, to promote athletic competition between the four houses, Taffy set up a running test. To my amazement and that of many of my peers, I succeeded in completing 880 yards inside two and a half minutes, along with other guys considered to be the best runners in the school.

In summer it was a different story! Cricket was the name of the game. Again, we played other schools in East Anglia. I must have been in about my second season, when I decided to cease cricket forthwith, as being a thoroughly nasty and vicious game! We used to play cricket at the back of the school in the summer evenings after homework was complete. In two successive sessions, I received bouncers right between the eyebrows. It was then that I joined the school sailing club, and spent many happy summers on the Orwell, sailing either tiny chine-hulled Cadets in school races, or the larger Dragonflies or GPs. The Dragonfly was a clinker-hulled class developed at Waldringfield on the nearby River Deben. Here too at Waldringfield I spent many happy weekends sailing with my cousins from Ipswich.

Mealtimes were a communal affair. The house master and the senior prefects would sit on the head table. The rest of us sat at the other tables, wherever we could find a chair. Before the meal started we would all stand. Grace would then be said, and we all sat down. I remember one hot summer when an enterprising pupil had flicked a pat of butter on to the ceiling above the head table. There was great mirth one day when it melted in the heat, and scored a bull's eye on the prefect sitting below.

The curriculum at Woolverstone was fairly standard, as grammar schools went in those days. We learnt the three Rs, together with history, geography, French and Latin, also music and divinity. The first big test came at 16, when we sat for our GCE 'O'-level exams, the school-leaving test for those who don't want to go on to university. Most of us took about six subjects. Somehow in aggregate I came out with the highest score, the academic dux of the school! It was no special thing in those days, although I remember getting a nice book as a prize. In addition to the formal teaching, I learnt to play the violin, and in the long summer holidays, attended two cycling trips to northern France.

We had a Young Farmer's Club at Woolverstone, where we learnt some of the basic aspects of farming and animal husbandry. Our involvement extended to keeping about six pigs, who were kept in a piggery close to the Woolverstone church. They were fed on the waste food from the school canteens, and it was the club members' job to heat it all up in a copper, and serve it to them when it had cooled down enough. One year the pigs acquired a stomach virus, and to our dismay they all died suddenly. There was an investigation by the Department of Agriculture, and thereafter we stopped keeping pigs. One other benefit of our membership was that we got free tickets to the Royal Agricultural shows held in Ipswich, and sometimes scored a brief part time job, leading gambolling cattle around the main ring. It was no joke to have a bull tread on your foot! Finally in the $6^{th}$ form, when the 'A' level exams were over, and we were waiting to leave school for good, we were allowed to go vegetable picking for nearby farmers, and make some pocket money.

Sixth form was a more serious phase of my schooldays. Most of us had a session with a careers officer who made a special visit to the school. Since the age of eight, when my mother had taken me to see the Geology Museum at Sandown on the Isle of Wight, I had wanted to become a geologist. There was something about those giant dinosaur's thigh bones on display, which as they say, got me "hooked"! So when perched in front of the careers officer, I knew exactly what I wanted to do. The officer gave me good advice, but it was not exactly what I wanted to hear. "Don't waste your time studying geology while at school", he said. "You must study maths, physics and chemistry at 'A' level, and get into university. They will teach you all your geology there". My best subjects till then had been the arts, with distinctions in French and History. I knew instinctively that the 'A' levels were going to be very hard work for me, especially chemistry, my worst subject. And so it was, but in my 'A' level results, which were very mediocre, my best result was in Chemistry! Fortunately, my results on average were not too bad. I scored an interview at Christ's College, Cambridge, but was told I could have a place only if I repeated my 'A' level exams next year, and got a better score. Since I had also been offered a firm immediate place at Imperial College, UK's foremost technological university, my choice was easy, and I enrolled for a degree in Mining Geology in London.

In the long summer holidays while in the sixth form I managed to get a part-time casual job as a packer for a pharmaceutical warehouse. Chemists shops would order various drugs and medical things like bandages. We would go to the warehouse shelves and select the ordered items which would then be parcelled up for despatch. At tea break I rapidly acquired the nick-name of 'Tin Guts'. This was because I could swallow a mug of piping hot tea in about half the time that it took the other guys. One of the supervisors asked me one day what I was going to do when I left school. "I'm going to go to university and get a degree in geology, and after that I'm going to travel the world and look for big mineral deposits", I said. The supervisor shook his head sadly and said "What you really need to do is to go and find a proper job like a bus driver or something, and get all these silly ideas out of your head!"

Looking back on my boarding school days, I can see how lucky we were to have had such wonderful, dedicated teachers, and the friendly relationship we had with them. Our maths master Mr Goetzee was the person I credit for getting me through 'A' level maths, and he was a devout Catholic. In the 6$^{th}$ form he invited me and a couple of my fellow students to have a sherry with him in his room. I forget the occasion but it must have been when the exams were over. On the wall of his room he had a graphic crucifix, with the bleeding body of Christ. I looked at this and thought how depressing it was to see it, and asked him if it didn't depress him also. "Not at all" he said. "It's a reminder that death awaits everyone of us, and that on our death we will face judgement about our actions in this life. So in our daily life we can try to make sure to avoid doing things that offend our own conscience".

4

# UNIVERSITY

In October 1960, I entered the Royal School of Mines (RSM) in Prince Consort Road, South Kensington as a Fresher. Within Imperial College, itself then part of the huge University of London, there were three constituent colleges at that time. These were the Royal School of Mines, the City & Guilds Institute (C&G), and the Royal College of Science (RCS). Each college had its own mascot. RSM's was a giant rubber "Michelin Man". C&G's was a gigantic spanner, and as for RCS, well I don't remember, and our main rivalry was with C&G. However, the general rivalry between the three colleges was high, and was celebrated not only on the sports field but also at the ritualistic Morphy Day pitched battle, which took place on the banks of the Thames near Putney. The objective of Morphy Day was to seize possession of "the Oar", or retain it if you were the current holders. The oar was a real oar, of which the exact ancestry I cannot remember. The real rivalry however was with "Them". They were the students from Camborne School of Mines, near Redruth in Cornwall. Annually, an epic rugby and other sports matches were played with these, our arch- rivals. The rugby match was played for "The Bottle", a huge green champagne bottle trophy which is still fought for every year, as I write. Sometimes the match was at Camborne, and on at least one occasion involved the two teams trying to play each other in a blizzard! Other years, it would be in London.

As an undergrad, I did not have much time or inclination for student union activities. Due to the fact that my parents lived on the very edge of London, I was considered to be a local student, and as such did not qualify for a place in a Hall of Residence. So my daily lot included three hours of travelling - an hour and a half each way. This was tiring as well as expensive, and so the famed life of parties and student pranks never really materialised for me. It was a major effort just to get my assignments done! So rather than get involved in the student night-life, I took advantage of the opportunity to continue playing rugby for RSM Seconds at Imperial College's Harlington grounds, and also joined the I.C. Underwater Club. The Underwater Club was the college's scuba diving group, and was a special branch of the British Sub-Aqua Club (BSAC). Our branch was well equipped and had dozens of tanks, an inflatable diving boat, its own compressor, and a lot of other equipment including diving suits. It also had its own Landrover vehicle, in which on weekends we would travel down to the Dorset coast for a dive, or even as far away as North Wales. Best of all, as BSAC members, we received all our instruction free once we had paid for our annual membership.

In 1960, scuba diving involved putting on a dry rubber suit which had seals at the neck, and wrists. Winter diving involved the purchase of some long-sleeved woolly vests and long johns! Sometimes we would dive in flooded gravel pits, which could be up to a hundred feet deep and have pitch black water. Diving in such conditions became a cheerful challenge, and we were secure in the knowledge that there would be no sharks waiting for us in the murky depths. Other times, on winter coastal dives, the best we could manage would be half an hour in the drink before surfacing with blue lips and numb fingers from a soup in which underwater visibility was only about one foot if we were lucky!

It was not long before we heard about the new neoprene rubber wet suits. In those days the first available neoprene only had a smooth skin on one side, and was about 4mm thick, but full of tiny cellular holes that made the suit buoyant. We would purchase a big sheet of the neoprene rubber and a pattern, then measure ourselves and cut out the shapes. The seams were then glued together with neoprene impact adhesive. If you wanted to be really fancy, you could stitch the seam for extra strength, and then cover it with some rubber tape. Wet suits were stretchy, two-piece affairs, and putting the zip in to the jacket was a real test of skill. One also had to be incredibly careful pulling the suit on and off, as the neoprene tore very easily. To dive in cold water, we would take a thermos flask of warm water, and having put the suit on, would pour the water between the suit and our skin. This made a real difference to your endurance if you were diving under the ice on a frozen lake, as I found one day at a lake called “Laughing Waters” in Buckinghamshire. Soon other improvements came, and double skin neoprene could be obtained. Today of course, a professionally made suit is a work of art, with coloured nylon cloth on each side as well as superbly fitted zips. But I still cringe at the cost of buying a professionally made suit, and would much prefer the challenge of making my own.

Studying at RSM was a satisfying period in my life, though physically hectic. In the long summer holidays, we were not allowed to take a rest. One trip included going down to Cornwall to the RSM’s very own mine at Tywarnhale on the north Cornwall coast. Here we learnt the fine points of both surface and underground surveying, as well as how to tell a good Cornish pastie from a bad one! We also leant the art of tying the two surveys together by means of “shaft plumbing!”. In our course at that time there were six of us, and until 2018 I was still in touch with three of them, namely Simon Rexworthy, Bob Garrett and Mike Seaward. We had a lot of fun and enjoyed the bracing Cornish weather. Another time, we went down near Penzance and Redruth again for spells doing field mapping and also practising applied geochemistry and applied geophysics over known mineral lode systems. On another working holiday, Simon and I went up to work for ICI at Billingham in County Durham. We had to do six weeks of practical underground mining shifts, and prepare a study report on our return. The ammonia and plaster plant at Billingham was sited right over the top of an anhydrite mine. The anhydrite, which occurred in thick beds, was a de-hydrated form of gypsum, and once mined and brought to the surface, was used for making gypsum for plaster-board and other building products. This intensely practical training was to serve me very well in my first job as a geologist.

Another memorable trip was at the end of my second year. As mining industry students, we were expected to go overseas and gain both some practical work experience and also some project data. So some of us went to Spain, another to Sierra Leone, some to South Africa, and I myself to north-west Turkey for three months, where I was lucky to visit many borate mines. The information collected was used to compile our Honours thesis for our Mining Geology degree.

The highlight of my third year once the final exams were over was to lead a diving expedition group of Underwater Club members to the island of Ibiza off the coast of Spain. The expedition was sponsored by the Royal Geographical Society and our aim was to collect marine life specimens from the sea floor between the southern end of Ibiza and a small but steep island called Vedra. We had also arranged to collaborate with a group from Birmingham University, who were doing a flora survey on the native plants growing on Ibiza. We travelled in the Underwater Club's trusted landrover with our trailer full of suitcases and diving equipment, taking the ferry from Dover to Dieppe in France, on to Paris where we picked up some sponsorship goods, then southwards and into Spain. Once in Spain we drove to Barcelona to pick up the ship that would ferry us to Ibiza.

The ship Ciudad de Ibiza.

There were 8 of us and we stayed initially in a small pension in Ibiza until meeting up with our expedition diving boat, a former lifeboat. Once all our equipment was on board we motored down to the south end of Ibiza and set up camp.

Isla Vedra, with the Birmingham University boat.

The expedition went very well, and we collected lots of specimens, all of which were pickled in formalin so that we could give them to The Natural History Museum which was very close to our college in London. The team members apart from myself were Simon Rexworthy, Deputy Leader, and Eric Sigurdson, Dudley Pinnock, Roger Pullin, Peter Jenkins, Terry Bowman and Bob Davis.

The diving expedition team (author second from right).

The water at the south end of Ibiza was crystal clear. From a dinghy we could look over the side and see our divers working on the sea floor one hundred feet below. The Birmingham University boat was close by, and they had a decompression chamber on board in case of diving decompression accidents, but fortunately we never needed to use it. I reached my own scuba diving depth record during this expedition, to a depth of 69m (deeper than 200 feet).

Unfortunately I did not get to travel back with the rest of the team at the end of our expedition, and had to leave early, with Simon our Deputy Leader being placed in charge of the return trip. An urgent telegram had arrived which told me that my father was very seriously ill in hospital, and that I should return immediately on a flight that had been booked to take me straight back to London.

# 5

# FINDING A JOB

College had finished and I had my honours degree in my pocket. But it was not a happy time in September 1963.

After returning from leading the scuba diving expedition in Spain, my mother and I visited my father regularly at the hospital in Great Portland Street, London. He was very gaunt, and was no longer able to speak. He had suffered an aneurysm of the aorta as a result of high blood pressure. At the time of this incident, he and my mother were visiting my Uncle Russell and his wife Barbara, and Russell being a GP immediately got him sent to a nearby hospital at Stoke Mandeville. Later he was transferred to the hospital at Great Portland Street in London. The surgeons there said that they couldn't operate on him, as they believed his kidneys would fail as he had advanced nephritis.

On one visit we were taken aside and told that he was like a man clinging by his finger nails to the edge of a precipice. Although we hoped and prayed for his recovery, it was clear that the surgeons believed he was going to die. And slowly he became more gaunt, and his skin became yellow, and he turned into a gibbering wreck.

It took him ten weeks to reach his release, and my mother was there with him when he died. My poor father was only 53 years old, and my mother was a widow at 50. We went to view his body after the post mortem, but could only see his face which was calm and relaxed. Then there was his cremation service, and his ashes were sprinkled in a garden of remembrance at Honour Oak. We had a wake back at our house in Lee, and my father's colleagues came and said what a wonderful and fair boss he had been. Then our relatives went back to their homes, as my mother and I tried to grasp the impact of our new situation.

My immediate priority was to find a job, as my mother now only had my father's pension to live on. There were little or no opportunities for geologists in UK at that time, unless you wanted to work at a coal mine for the National Coal Board. I applied for two jobs, one with the Tanganyka Geological Survey, and another with the Ghana State Mining Corporation, and managed to get an interview for both. An offer came in for the position in Ghana first, which was as Mine Geologist at the Bibiani Gold Mine. I delayed for several weeks as I wanted to see if I would get an offer for Tanganyka as well, but not being confident that I would get a second offer, I accepted the job in Ghana. A few days later of course, an offer for Tanganyka did come in, and it was slightly better. I was tempted to pull out of my Ghana acceptance, but then decided to honour it.

Looking back, I can see that this was a critical decision point in my life. Had I accepted the job in Tanganyka instead, the whole of my life from then on would have been completely different. Nevertheless, I have no regrets.

My next immediate dilemma was about leaving my mother to fend for herself, but she encouraged me to take the job. Her brothers and sisters and their families were only a phone call away, and we could keep in touch by letters.

# 6

# CULTURE SHOCK

I arrived by plane at Accra, the capital of Ghana on a hot day. I had flown out from London to start my professional career as a Mine Geologist.

Along with the other passengers we collected our luggage and went through customs. At the exit there was no friendly person holding a board with my name on it, so I went outside and stood in the hot sun. A string of taxis came and went, and after about an hour I accepted the fact that there was no one coming to meet me.

Further passengers started arriving to pick up another flight, and I grabbed one of the taxis and asked to be taken to the Bibiani Gold Mine. It was about 160 miles away to the north-west, so the taxi driver was very happy to pick up such a large fare.

We arrived eventually at the mine and had to wait at the security gate, while the Mine Security Manager came down to check. As I had not enough money with me, he kindly paid the taxi driver and took me to my allocated bungalow, which fortunately had been prepared in advance. So began my one year contract with the Ghana State Mining Corporation in October 1963, as the Mining Geologist, reporting directly to the Mine Manager. With the exception of the Ghanaian Security Manager, all of the management team were expats, mainly from Britain and a few from Italy, plus some Anglo-Indian shift bosses who were in charge in the mill.

Mack, the Canadian Mine Captain, became a good friend and confident. In this, my very first job straight out of university, I was very fortunate. My training back at the college in London had been so thorough that I was able to handle all of my duties at an operating underground gold mine.

Bibiani had been a British company originally - Bibiani 1927 Ltd. The accommodation bungalows were up on a hill, at the top of which a very tall mahogany tree stood, the Bibiani tree. The legend was that as long as the Bibiani tree kept standing, the mine would keep operating. Close to the top of the hill was the mine manager's bungalow. Below the bungalows was the golf course, and at the bottom of the golf course was the Club House, which featured a pleasant bar, a swimming pool and a lending library. There was a small hospital on site, managed by a friendly Dutch doctor who had been in Irian Jaya while Indonesia was still under Dutch control.

My own bungalow had the bare essentials - a kitchen with a small fridge, a tiny bathroom and toilet, the bedroom complete with mosquito net, and a front lounge with some armchairs and a desk. Heavy wooden louvered wooden shutters covered the windows, which was just as well, because the diagonal diamond-patterned metal window grids carried no panes of glass, and at night a stream of mosquitoes gained easy access. So writing home was usually done sitting on my bed underneath the mosquito net. The house was a duplex, and on the other side of the dividing wall lived Nap, an Italian shift boss who was a friendly character.

Our water came from an abandoned shaft at the north end of the mine, and this water had to be boiled for 15 minutes and then poured into a ceramic filter vessel. This had two porous ceramic candles sticking up from the floor of the chamber, and through which he boiled water would filter, to fill up a lower chamber from which our water for drinking and cooking could be tapped. We took anti-malarial tablets but in addition to malaria there were active yellow fever mosquitoes. Other diseases like bilharzia, sleeping sickness, yaws, elephantiasis and TB were rife. Before independence the country was known as the Gold Coast, with a chilling nick name, The White Man's Grave.

A houseboy was arranged for me, a young Kanjarga tribesman from the north of Ghana, whose name was Solomon. Out of my monthly salary of 90 British pounds I would pay him 12 pounds per month. He prepared my meals and did my washing and ironing, and kept the bungalow swept and clean. He also did the local shopping for fruits and vegetables. His English was good, and he taught me a few words of Twi, the local dialect.

One day in November 1963 when I got back from the mine office, I was met by Solomon who was crying. "Oh Master, something terrible has just happened!" he said. He had heard on the radio that President Kennedy of the USA had just been assassinated in Dallas. I had a small portable record player, and at night I would play some of the Beatles' LP records that I had bought with me. Now whenever I hear some of those old Beatles' songs, I think of November 1963 and the assassination of Kennedy.

Often in the evenings I would go down to the club house for a drink and to socialise with the other expats. The bar was magnificent, with a high, flat top surface made of a single plank of rich red varnished mahogany. Patrons could sit at the bar on high stools, or against the back wall on comfortable divans. On one of my earliest visits I was having the social layout at the mine explained to me as I sat at the bar, and apparently there were two cliques at the mine, the 'we love the mine manager' group and the 'we don't like the mine manager' group. Anyway, while I was sitting there, I noticed a black ring spoiling the mahogany surface of the bar right at the point where I sat.

"What a shame" I said, and my companion told me there was a story to this black ring. Apparently a young English metallurgist had secured a position in the gold recovery plant, and he had lived in the same bungalow where I was now living. Apparently at his company medical, the examining doctor had written that in his opinion, although physically fit, the candidate was not suited for work in the tropics. Anyway, his job application was accepted and he duly arrived at the mine, but did not last long. One night he came to the club and asked for a glass of water, which he placed on the bar in front of him. He then pulled a small piece of folded paper out from his shirt pocket, took out a small white lump and dropped it into his glass and watched it dissolve.

He then drank the glass of water and fell back off his stool, dead! He had committed suicide by taking sodium cyanide he had obtained from the gold plant. The cyanide solution that dribbled from his glass had burnt the black ring!

The staff bungalows could be accessed by a network of concrete paths, but at night there was no lighting so it was easy to get lost at first. The paths were patrolled by the mine security force, Ghanaians who wore a uniform which included a smart red fez hat. They were there to stop villagers from the hills coming down to steal from the bungalows. At night it was easy to bump into them due to the lack of lighting, although usually they would hear you coming and say "All correct, Master!" If the moon was shining you could see the whites of their eyes and the gleam of their teeth.

An amusing story was told to me by the Chief Chemist, whose name was Dick. His wife had lived with him on site for a few years, and one very hot night close to the end of the dry season, her skin was suffering from prickly heat. With lights off in the house, they heard the pitter patter on the roof of the first rain signalling the start of the wet season. Opening the French doors to the balcony, she went out and stood there naked in the dark to feel the rain falling on her skin, only to be greeted by a voice from the path below ......"All correct, Madam"!

Dick told me another story about how he would make his tea in a laboratory beaker, only to be called out of his office to attend to some matter in another part of the mine complex. Often when he came back, his tea beaker would be half drunk, or completely empty. He figured that one of his Ghanaian lab assistants was drinking the tea. So one day he made his beaker of tea as usual, but then jumped up and said he remembered he had to go to a meeting in the main office, and walked out. Sure enough, when he returned his tea had been drunk again, but he said nothing and simply made himself another one.

The next few days, one of his assistants was missing. Then on the third day the assistant, whose name was Khofi, came back. Dick asked him why he had been absent, and he replied "Oh Master, me shit plenty too much! "Right" said Dick, "don't drink my tea again"! What Dick had done was to lace the tea with a very small amount of a chemical indicator solution used in the lab, called phenolpthalein. This chemical just happens to be a very powerful laxative!

A favourite social activity on the weekends was golf competitions, sometimes held away at other gold mine sites. I bought a second-hand set of clubs and had a go, with a handicap of 24. My favourite trick on the very first drive with a new ball was to make a deep smiley cut in the skin of the ball, which would then go screaming away on a big curve into the rough. In the competitions for a small silver spoon, a secondary competition developed amongst the other players, whose ambition was to be my partner. It turned out that my partners were so cheered up by my endless mistakes that generally it was my partner who won the competition! The last time I ever played golf was many years later, in Indonesia, where I was on a consulting trip. It was one of those horrible courses where many fairways were dissected two or three times by a seemingly endless series of small lakes. Just as well that second-hand balls recovered from the water traps were cheap. I lost nine balls on the first nine holes going out, and another nine balls on the way back.

The Ghanaians were very keen to be educated. For a short while I taught geography in the evenings at a local school. The students were preparing to sit for the British GCE 'O' Level exam in Geography. They were amazingly keen and there was no chatting or skylarking. You could hear a pin drop while I explained to them about the tilt of the earth's axis and how this created the seasons with the summer and winter solstices and the equinoxes in between.

Every so often the tribesmen would have a big get together. As well as the local Ashanti tribesmen, the mine employed other Ghanaians from all over Ghana. They would have spectacular drumming displays using drumsticks that were bent over at the end.

Tribal celebrations at Bibiani

The local Paramount Chief at Bibiani while I was there was a British guy who had married a local Ashanti woman. In accord with local custom, he maintained a little mini Pixie House, where he would make food offerings to the spirits. Another custom was to pour libations of wine onto the ground to appease the spirits.

For the local villagers at Bibiani, a green banana species called plantain was a staple part of the diet. These plantains were not sweet like a banana. They were prepared by pounding the plantain flesh in a narrow wooden pot to make a kind of dough that was then cooked, a meal called fufu. Another item of the diet was cassava, a long brown-skinned root that grew horizontally in the ground below the parent canes. As it was not always possible for the expats to buy the potatoes we were used to from the market in Kumasi, the nearest big town, we used to eat cassava instead. Although its taste was different to potato, it was a quite acceptable alternative.

In the garden of my bungalow was a huge leafy avocado tree. Never having eaten them while growing up in UK, I did not pay them any attention. They were probably eaten by the local wildlife which included Agama Lizards, that were everywhere outside. They would run fast, then stop and bob their orange heads up and down.

On part of the mine lease not far from the expat bungalows was an old open cut mine called Big Mug, where gold ore close to the ground surface had been dug out and removed.

I used to go and sit there with my binoculars on some of the weekend breaks to watch the local bird life, including kites and buzzards.

After about nine months at Bibiani I was transferred to an alluvial diamond mine on the Birim River at a place called Takrowase, near Akim Oda. The diamonds were in gravel beds on the flood plain of the river. There was a light forest cover and in places cocoa farmers had planted their cocoa trees in the shade underneath the main canopy. To access the diamonds the forest trees had to be cut down and removed. Power shovels would then remove the gravel layers which had been previously assessed by sampling the area with a network of 6 ft diameter pits which went down about thirty feet to the soft clayey bedrock. Each pit was deepened one foot at a time, the gravel spoil being taken to a testing wash site where the gravel was screened and concentrated so that the diamonds could be recovered and weighed from each foot of removed spoil. The grade of each layer was recorded as carats per cubic yard, and the results were shown on cross-section drawings, so that the mining crews would know which layers were barren and which layers contained a mineable grade of diamonds.

At Takrowase the expat accommodation was in a clearing about one mile from the mining area. It had been put there by a Dutch company that had previously owned the lease. The Dutchmen were clearly there for only one purpose, which was to work. So there was no club house, no golf course and no swimming pool.

There were about six bungalows only and some of the senior Ghanaian mining staff lived there as well as myself and an elderly metallurgist, Bill Glennie, who was the Concentrator Superintendent. Our water was rainwater that was channelled into an underground concrete bunker, and had to be hand-pumped up to a tank to supply the bungalow. The hot water for the shower was in a 44-gallon drum painted black, set up on the roof. In the sun it became extremely hot. There was a fan set in the ceiling of each room, and fly wire over the windows to keep the mosquitoes out. The front door also had a fly wire screen, but unfortunately it had a gap at the bottom, so quite a few mosquitoes would get in. It was too hot for sleeping under a mosquito net, so I used to sleep naked without a top sheet over me. The local mosquitoes were very greedy and would suck blood until they were too fat to fly off. So in the morning when I woke up there would be little red splats all over the sheet where I had rolled over in the night and squashed them.

Bill had previously worked at the Bawdwin lead-zinc mine in northern Burma. The mine was very isolated and in an area where the local tribesmen used to regularly ambush any government convoys that came through to the mine with supplies from Rangoon. The tribesmen had muzzle loading rifles. When they started firing at the concentrator, the staff would lie down between the banks of flotation tanks to avoid being hit. When the tribesmen ran out of lead balls, they would fire near-spherical garnet crystals instead!

At Takrowase we were deep in Ashanti territory. My Kanjarga house boy Solomon had insisted on coming with me, and the locals gave him a hard time, overcharging him for the food that he bought. He had to live in a one room unit that initially had no fly wire until I got it installed for him. At night we could hear talking drums - a brief throb in one direction followed by perhaps a longer burst from another direction, and then further drum throbs from yet another direction.

Illegal miners had a sixth sense for where the richest diamond-bearing gravels were. They would move in at night in places where there was little or no overburden and pick the area clean, working by the light of hurricane lamps. If you happened to come across them it was best to retreat quickly before they could catch and kill you.

The diamonds were recovered by jigs, a machine in which the gravel is fed over a screen which pulsates up and down in a water-filled tank. At the richer diamond mine upstream at CAST (Consolidated African Selection Trust), some jigs had blocked holes in their screens, and diamonds escaped into the tailings or waste. However, this waste was collected and stockpiled inside a special security enclosure that was a few miles away from the main plant and connected to it by a short railway track. Special hand driven railway carts were arranged and a team of men assembled to go to the security enclosure, load up and bring the gravel back to the main plant for re-treatment. The men were timed in and out of each area as the gravel was transferred. A week late, all the men in the transfer team had brand new Vespa motor scooters, so in the journey back to the main plant that had found to time to hand-pick a tidy number of diamonds.

At Takrowase I used to weigh the recovered diamonds in a small shed that was locked at night. The shed was regularly broken into in the hope that I may have left some diamonds in there.

On another occasion the Plant Superintendent, Bill Glennie, was pulling his hair out because hardly any concentrate had been recovered. Then a few mornings later a Nigerian who had a diggers licence which enabled his men to re-work the plant tailings was walking through the bush and found a local man handpicking diamonds from a plastic dustbin full of concentrate that had been stolen from the plant concentrate area at night. Some crooked security guys had left the gates of the concentrate area unlocked briefly so their mates could get in. The Nigerian grabbed this man, and the police were called. They arrested the man and took him away. An hour later he was out of jail on 20,00 pounds bail! He obviously had some very powerful friends.

After three months at Takrowase, it was time for me to go on my annual leave, and as an underground worker I had three months. I decided that although diamonds were fascinating, the problems arising from having to work on this isolated site with zero amenities were not a justification for renewing my contract, and I returned to London.

# 7

# BACK TO ENGLAND, BUT ONLY FOR A WHILE

Back in England, I returned to living with my mother at her house in Lee. For the first six months I felt as if I was shivering inside, even when the weather was quite warm.

I got a job with a geophysical exploration company who were using marine seismic exploration to discover the dome structures in the rocks below the floor of the North Sea that could indicate structures that might be trapping oil and gas deposits. The job was based in Croydon, about an hour on the bus from Lee. The company went on to make some big discoveries.

At university I had become a fan of folk music, and was excited when some famous folk singers gave a performance in Croydon which I was able to attend. There was the Canadian Indian singer, Buffy Saint Marie together with Rambling Jack Elliot, and Julie Felix, a British folk singer. I still listen to Buffy today, although her style has changed dramatically since her early folk singing days.

Processing marine seismic records was a worthwhile and valuable activity, but did not enthuse me as much as scrambling over rocky outcrops of ore. So in early July 1965 I accepted a job with Conzinc Riotinto of Australia (CRA), nominally based in Melbourne, and they gave me a week in Iran on the way out to check out a borate mineral prospect in the southern desert.

# 8

# PAPUA NEW GUINEA AND THE SOLOMONS

I had managed to get the job with CRA, which I thought was going to be based in Australia through a contact in the London Office of Rio Finex, a subsidiary of the mining giant Rio Tinto. They knew that I had spent some time in Turkey working on borates and had written my thesis for my Honours degree in Mining Geology based on that work. So as a bonus I was given an auxiliary trip to Iran, where I would meet up with their Exploration Manager, Tony Warren.

Arriving in Teheran I was given a room at the Teheran Hilton, from where one could see a stunning view of the Elburz Mountains to the north. Even in summer some traces of snow could still be seen at the top. Arrangements had been made for a trip to the far south of Iran to look at a borate prospect in the desert. Meanwhile there was a chance to see the spectacular Iranian crown jewels, that were held in the basement of one of the main banks, and open for visitors to see.

This year the Shah was still in power, and around the open-air swimming pool were ladies in bikinis, sipping their cocktails.

The day of our trip came and we flew to Isfahan, and had a glimpse of the famous Blue Mosque.

From Isfahan we flew to Yadz, where we were to pickup a landrover for a further road trip to Shahrbabak. While in the plane, the landscape below us was something like the moon, with the interesting difference that often holes could be seen stretching in a line from the base of mountains over to small towns and villages.

Iranian desert scene

These strange holes were actually wells, called qanats, and they each joined up to an underground tunnel that allowed spring water from the hills to be carried safely under the desert, sometimes for hundreds of kilometres to where the water was needed. The technology was thousands of years old, and there are a type of fish living there that have become completely blind, through living so long in complete darkness.

At Shahrbabak, the site of the borates was a nearly flat plain. Some silky white fibrous minerals had been discovered in a pit dug for water, and this white mineral was ulexite, a sodium-calcium hydrated borate. The mineral had crystallised there as a result of boron in the ground water. The temperature was very high, I estimate around 45° C, and the whole landscape shimmered in the heat coming from the ground. The metal on the landrover was too hot to touch. Nearby were some shallow nomad tents, with about six layers of blanket to stop the heat from penetrating. There was no sign of any rock outcrop, but there may have been borate bearing sediments below the ground surface of course, although trenching and possibly even drilling would be required to investigate this.

Ulexite mineralisation

We returned to Yadz and Isfahan, then back to Teheran where I caught an onward flight to Australia via Bangkok.

My first landfall in Australia was in Brisbane in the early afternoon on Friday July 29th, 1965. My destination was in Melbourne however.

I was having a beer with a fellow passenger when he left to catch a plane to Sydney, and I wondered why my flight had not also been called and went to the enquiries desk. It seemed my plane had taxied from the international part of the airport to the domestic part! I got there just in time to see my plane taking off, complete with my jacket and luggage! I went again to the enquiry desk and was given a ticket for the next flight to Melbourne, which left about an hour later.

When I arrived in Melbourne I went to the luggage hall and of course, no sign of my luggage. So I went to the lost luggage counter, where I was given my jacket, and told that unfortunately my luggage was now in customs bond! "Well get it back out then" I fumed, only to be told that unfortunately this was not possible as it being Friday evening, the customs men had gone home for the weekend. I would have to come back on Monday morning! So yes, I remember it well - Friday, July 29$^{th}$, 1965!

I caught a taxi into Melbourne, to the Victoria Hotel in Little Collins Street. I had short trousers on, shoes and long white socks, and a short- sleeved shirt. Being still the middle of the Australian winter, it was cold and there was a continuous light drizzle of rain. I shivered in my room most of the weekend, and was kept awake for two nights by a kamikaze mosquito who dived bombed me close to my ear whenever I nodded off to sleep. To make things worse, the Victoria was the only temperance hotel in Melbourne, and I couldn't buy myself a beer!

On the Monday morning I made my way to the CRA office that was close by in Collins Street, where I was met by Don Carruthers, CRA's Exploration Manager. "You're a lucky guy, Mike" said Don. "We're sending you to Bougainville in Papua New Guinea, a great new copper project where you'll be able to do your mapping, and every three months we'll fly you back to Melbourne and you can draw up your maps here in the air conditioning of head office!" It all sounded wonderful. I then got leave to go out to the airport and get my luggage cleared through customs. I picked up what information I could about my new assignment, and a few days later I flew off to the capital of PNG in Port Moresby, then to Rabaul at the east end of New Britain island, and then in a small DC3 aircraft to Kieta at the southern end of Bougainville island. I was almost the only passenger, and the others were met by local Bougainvilleans who took them away on motorbikes.

The Kieta airstrip was just a green field by the edge of the beach, with jungle on the other side. I found a tree and sat in the shade with my suitcase. It quickly dawned on me that no one was coming to pick me up. A local lorry came though the field and I hailed it, and the driver gave me a lift into Kieta, and dropped me at the Kieta Hotel. After a quick beer I asked about the whereabouts of the CRA Office. It was in a bungalow just down the road, and I walked over there. I knocked at the front door, which was open, and went in. A guy was sprawled over the desk, asleep. I coughed gently and he woke up. "Yes Mate, what can I do for you?" he asked. I explained that I was the new geologist from Melbourne. "Aw, shit Mate, nobody told us you were coming!"

They gave me a room in the Kieta pub, and the next morning I met Dave Binnie, the ex-British Fleet Air Arm pilot who was to take me up to the mine camp site at Barapena, in a valley on the other side of the mountains. My luggage was strapped on to the skids of the 2-man chopper, a Bell G47. We took off and went up in a steep climb, steeper and steeper, until our backs were horizontal with the chopper's nose sticking straight up vertically. At this point Dave beat loudly on his chest with one fist, giving his imitation of the roar of an Aberdeen Angus bull. He then flicked the tail straight up so that we were now facing straight down to the ground, which was approaching rapidly. Down we went and I was quite relieved when he pulled out into level flight! "Wow, Dave" I said, "that was terrific - can we do that again?" From then onwards we were great friends, as he was greatly impressed by the fact that I had not chundered my breakfast into my lap!

At Barapena there were several other geologists including Phil Macnarama who had come to Bougainville from the famous Tom Price iron ore mine, and some field assistants. Other young geologists that passed through included, Tony Osman, Russell Fountain, and Tony Woodhill. Dick Spratt came as Senior Geologist and the famous Frank Hughes was also on site for a while. In charge of the Barapena camp was Rex Brooks, a young Australian who operated the daily radio back to Kobuan on the coast, where the main CRA administrative team were based. Rex ordered all the food and supplies, which was not just for us, but also for the local Bougainvillean men who worked for us and were paid some cash wages plus an amount of rice, tinned pilchards and some sticks of rum-soaked tobacco.

The manager of the Bougainville copper mine development at this early stage was Ken Phillips, a great boss and a very skilful mineral exploration geologist. It was his team that found the deposit by doing stream sediment sampling all the way up from the mouth of the Kawerong River that discharges into the sea on the south-west coast of Bougainville.

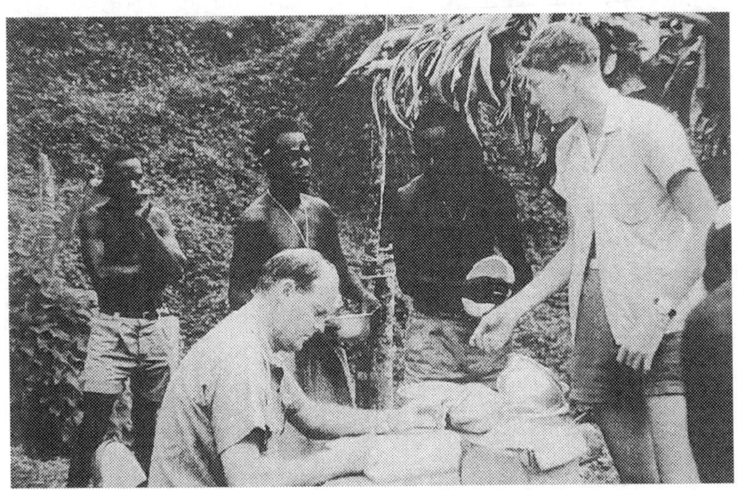

Ken Phillips and Rex Brooks at Barapena.

All our food was flown up to Barapena by helicopter, whenever the weather permitted it! Our family mail, the beer supplies, equipment, and in fact everything came in or went out only by helicopter. For heavy equipment like drilling machines, a big Sikorsky helicopter was available, and later we also got an Iroquois jet helicopter, of the type made famous by the TV serial MASH about the Vietnam war.

Bell helicopter taking off from Barapena

Flying choppers over tropical rainforests is a risky business, as there is very little open ground on which to land if engine trouble develops. The pilots have to practice an auto-rotate landing, necessitated if the tail rotor suffers damage while in flight. The tail rotor is the only thing that allows the chopper to fly straight. If the tail rotor fails, the pilot has to immediately disconnect the main rotor from the engine, otherwise the whole fuselage will rotate like the blades but in the opposite direction. The main rotor is feathered to allow a rapid descent on to a selected patch of clear ground. Just before impact the pilot increases the pitch of the blades to increase the lift and soften the landing. During my two years in PNG, three of the small Bell helicopters were written off through accidents, which in one case also killed the pilot when he crash-landed in heavy jungle having run out of fuel.

The Sikorsky in its hangar at Kobuan

Even the big Sikorsky also crashed. It was coming in slowly at Kobuan in stormy weather, when a down gust caused the Sikorsky's tail rotor to hit the edge of the hangar. The main rotor blades were then ripped off as the chopper hit the ground, leaving the chopper on its side with the engine still running and a pool of fuel on the ground. Rescuers had to use an axe to get the door open and pull the pilot out, who was badly bruised but otherwise unhurt.

Up in the mountains we had convectional rainfall and almost every day between about 9 am and 11 am there was a torrential downpour. Annual rainfall was in excess of 250 inches a year. On one occasion while I was there, it rained continuously for eight days. At such times when the surrounding peaks and high ridges were covered by low cloud, no helicopters were allowed in or out. Fortunately we had a large food store, and I became accustomed to my regular lunch consisting of a tin of mixed diced vegetables and a small tin of salmon.

Our bread did not last long. The first day a new loaf was taken out of the freezer, we would each have a few slices. In the humid air, green mould grew quickly, and we would slice off the mouldy outside of the loaf and cut more slices to eat. By about the 3rd day there was only a 2 inch cube left!

The true Bougainvilleans have very black skin, blacker than Africans, and tight curly hair. They were masters with a machete and an axe. With just a machete they could make very short work of a decent sized tree. The lingua franca in our dealings with the locals was Pidgin, which sounds a bit like baby-talk, sprinkled with German words from the days when Bougainville and the rest of PNG was part of a German protectorate before Australia took control. Ethnically they are closely aligned with the Solomon Islanders, rather than the Papua New Guineans. The population of Papua New Guinea consists of many different tribes, including long haired mainland Papuans and curly haired Melanesian people from the surrounding islands.

The local people had a village at Moroni, close by to the Barapena Camp. The village was right at the apex of a steep hill, a strategic position since it could be defended from all sides. On the slopes below the village there were gardens where they grew yams. They would shoot the flying fox bats, and also had their pigs that they would eat when they had a tribal celebration or 'sing sing'. There were very few birds in the Bougainville forests, but some of the trees had resident possums called 'kapoon' in Pidgin. If they believed there was a kapoon in residence, they would cut down a huge tree to catch it. Water came from the Kawerong river down in the valley below, at Barapena camp level. The women would have to walk down each day with their water pots, then carry them laboriously back up the steep hill to their village.

Maroni village

The old man of Maroni

My first job at Barapena was to take a team of local men with machetes and axes for line cutting through the jungle. Once a clear line was cut on a particular compass bearing, we would go back with a tape measure and every one hundred feet we would put in a wooden stake which carried a little aluminium tag with a number on it. At each tagged position we would put down a hole using a soil auger. At each point the soil from the surface to a depth of three feet would be put into a numbered bag. We would then twist the auger down for a second three feet, the sample again going into a bag with the depth and position marked. The position of each auger hole would be picked up by a surveyor who would put a little concrete cylinder in with a survey number marked on it. All the soil samples from the parallel lines cut through the jungle slopes would go down to the coast at Kobuan where we had a geochemist who would do cold-extractable copper analyses on each sample. The residue would be sent back to Australia for full chemical analysis. Once the results were available, a scaled map drawing would be prepared showing the survey lines, the sampling points and the copper values at each point. These values could then be contoured, so we knew exactly where the richest copper values in the soil were. That area would then be cleared of trees, a flat drilling pad prepared, and a drill rig would be brought in and set up.

Augering in progress

Another part of my job was to log the drill cores from the diamond drilling rigs. Logging involved identifying the rock type, describing the mineral veins intersected by the drill core, and their nature, for example barren quartz or carbonate, or quartz carrying visible copper minerals of different types. The depth of each part of the core was known since once the core barrel had been emptied into the core tray, a little wooden block was placed in the tray with the depth reached written in by the drillers. The diamond drill had a core barrel about 6 feet long, which at its bottom end has a tubular bit screwed on. The annular face of the bit was made out of a hard alloy which had abrasive diamonds set into it. It is these abrasive diamonds that do the cutting, and when they have abraded away, the old bit has to be replaced by a new one.

A diamond drilling core tray

As the drill string was rotated by the drill engine, the rotating bit pushed down into the rock, and a cylindrical drill core pushed up inside the core barrel. Each drill was manned by two men, a driller and his offsider. They camped in the jungle close to their rig. They also had some Bougainvillean assistants, one of whom was often perched at the top of the rig when the drill pipes were being pulled up to recover the contents of a full core barrel, and again when the pipes were being screwed back together for the empty core barrel to go back down the hole again. Around 1967 we got some new wireline drill equipment in. The wireline system enabled the full core barrel to be pulled up to the surface inside the drill rods, eliminating the lengthy unscrewing of the whole string of drill rods when the full core barrel needed to be brought up, and their re-screwing when the drill string went back down the hole again.

Bougainville Men working on top of a drill rig

The Bougainville society is matriarchal, meaning that the land is owned and passed on by the women. A consequence of our line cutting was to have to pay compensation almost every day to local tribesman who would present themselves to Rex Brooks early in the morning and say "Yu pella cutim diwai bilong mi" meaning "you have cut my tree down." Each tree had a value of ten shillings, so the money would be paid and the recipient would put his thumb print in the receipt book. Later the same day another two guys would rock up and ask to be paid for the same tree. It was easier to pay them than to argue.

My interest in nature served me well while up in the mountains at Barapena. There were a host of brilliant and large butterflies, including some blue and some bright yellow and green. There were also huge colourful spiders that would build their web across any available narrow track. There were some incredibly long and very narrow tube worms that lived in the soil. There were also occasional clumps of a beautiful pale purple flower on long stems that was actually an orchid called Spathoglottis, together with other less spectacular orchids that would grow in the forks of trees. In our accommodation we would occasionally be visited by long tropical centipedes that would slither along the top of the exposed overhead cross-beams. They had a very poisonous bite and whenever possible we would dispatch them with a machete.

Down on the coast at Kobuan our geochemist had his laboratory. Nick was from Yugoslavia and had a thick accent. As well as producing our preliminary copper assays he also had a magnificent collection of tropical seashells. The trick was to get them while they were still alive, and you could catch them by wading out on a calm night into the sea, with a powerful torch in your hand. At dusk the shell fish that have been hiding down in the sand during the day come out on the seabed and start looking for food, and can be seen moving around. Nick had Eggshell Cowries, Tiger Cowries and some of the poisonous Cone shells, together with long-tailed Murex shells and many other beautiful species. Once caught they would be left in an empty bucket where they died and started to rot. They were then very carefully picked out and placed near an ants' nest and the ants would clean them out. The need to pick them up carefully was because in the rotting process a copious liquid was produced with a terrible smell. If by chance some of this juice spilt onto your fingers, no amount of scrubbing would take the smell away! And you would smell it every time you brought your hand close to your nose for about the next week.

They say that time flies when you're having fun, and anyway, looking back it **was** fun. At any rate it was nine months before I got down to the coast at Kieta to have a swim. So much for Don Carruthers and his promise to have me back in Melbourne every three months! When I did get some real leave, it was normally only back to Rabaul for a week, where I used to stay at the Malaguna Hotel on Mango Avenue, and I also received two weeks annual leave back to Melbourne every year.

Our total dependence on helicopter transport did not last forever. The famous Snowy Mountain engineering group that had built the Snowy Mountains hydroelectric scheme in Australia was contracted to put in an access road from Kieta to the deposit, reaching the valley floor on the west side of the mountains at Barapena. "No worries" they said. "We will have it through in six weeks!" But it actually took more than six months before the road got through. The problem was that much of the ground in which the forest cover grew was covered by a layer of organically rich but still very soft volcanic ash, a crystal tuff that could easily be trenched with a spade. Once the trees were bulldozed down, the track cut by the dozers on the hillside slopes was almost immediately washed away by the daily convectional rainfall.

Layers in volcanic ash (crystal tuff)

The initial track had to be repeatedly cut back and down until it was going through moderately stable rock. On one occasion a dozer accidently went over the edge, and rolled slowly down the slope of fresh spoil right to the edge of the river below. Miraculously the driver was able to walk around the cabin as the dozer rolled, and get out unhurt at the bottom.

CRA had the very best intentions, and they took a group of the smartest villagers who worked for the exploration team and spoke the best English for a trip to the established and famous lead-zinc mines at Broken Hill in New South Wales. While they were there, the mining unions in Broken Hill also got to meet the Bougainvilleans, and shared a few of their strategies with them. The next thing we knew, the local tribesmen who lived in the Maroni village overlooking Barapena, complained to the Kiep (the local Australian administration Officer) that the noise of the bulldozers had made their pigs either commit suicide (meaning they had actually been killed and eaten), or that they had run away to the coast down the new road! To counteract this, CRA had to pay compensation for the pigs that had supposedly run away, and also had to fence both sides of the road for about 30 kilometres all the way back to the Arawa copra plantation!

A pig destined for the feast

As well as my time on Bougainville, I spent about six months on the CRAE Star, CRA's exploration vessel. It was a converted Japanese fishing vessel, 100 feet long, with a modified fold-down mast and a chopper pad on the back. The refrigerated fishing hold was still there, and we used to keep the 5 feet long mackeral that we used to catch down there.

A 5 ft long mackeral.

The CRAE Star team included Archie the captain, the chopper pilot and his engineer, Ian Whitcher the on-board Exploration Manager, Rudi Claric and myself as geologists, and Edgar Mucenikas our geochemist. We also had Bruce our field assistant, and the ship's islander crew including the Chief Engineer and the Ship's Mate, plus about four other Islander assistants, including the cook. We did stream sediment sampling of all the rivers on the northern PNG coast, from Madang all the way up almost to Vanimo on the then

Irian Jaya border. At Wewak there was still an intact Japanese Zero aircraft on the airport tarmac, left there after WWII.

Ian was a great leader for our exploration efforts. From university days his nick-name was "Witchetty Grub", based on the wood-boring moth grubs that are prized by Aboriginal people in Australia due to their nutritional value. He was one of the co-discoverers of the massive high grade iron ore deposit at the Tom Price mine in Western Australia.

The helicopter based on board the ship was always equipped with long cylindrical floats instead of the skids on each side that were standard for flights over land. While on board a lot of our diet consisted of tinned or frozen food, but we augmented this with fresh fish that we caught from the ship at night, vegetables that we bought from the villagers, and also crayfish that we obtained from the coastal villagers. Our islander crew also had traditional pacific island meals at times, including turtles and even flying foxes ('blak bokus' in pidgin). A rare delicacy for them was coconut crab, a land based crab that would climb coconut trees and could cut though the thick outer coconut husk to get at the white meat in the coconut inside.

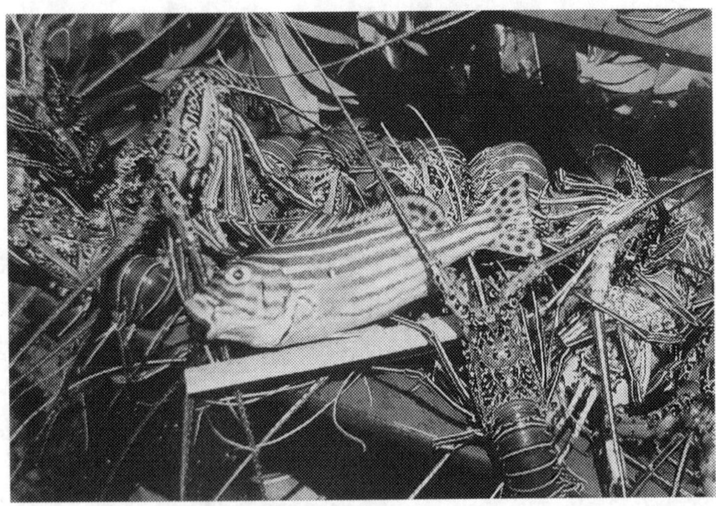

Crayfish and a Sweetlips

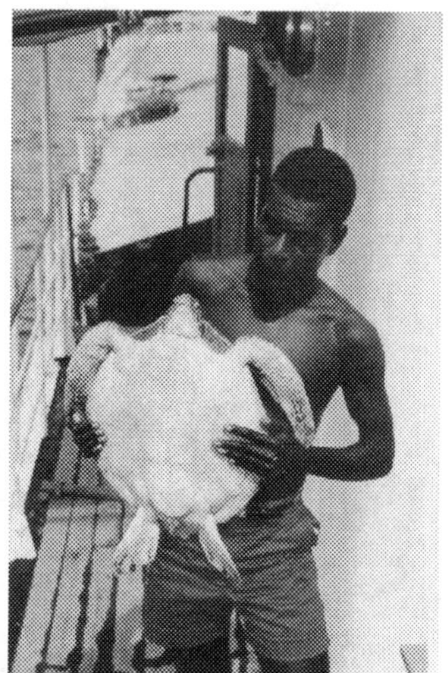

Turtle

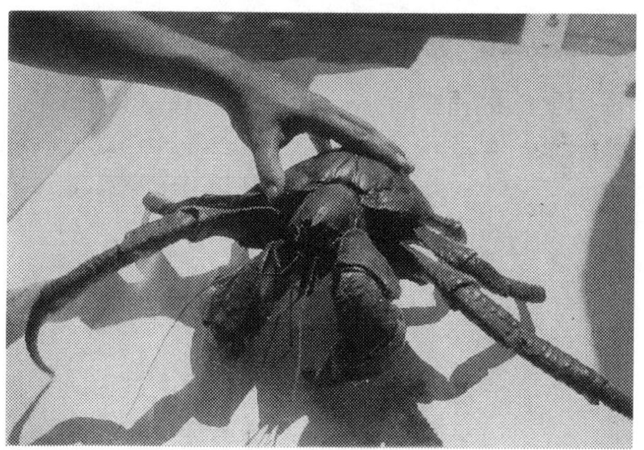

Coconot Crab

About 42 miles due west of Wewak we took a look at the area around Maprik, where platinum group minerals were apparently panned from river sands by the local people. Maprik had an Australian administration post based there, and the golf course doubled up as the airstrip for light planes. At Maprik we stayed several nights in the local motel, and I was able to buy a beautifully made carving of a crocodile ('pokpok' in pidgin) which was intended to be a child's toy. Between its jaws was a carved little man! The houses in the Maprik area were not on stilts, but had thick sloping thatch roofs that went all the way to the ground.

Maprik houses.

The local tribes had initiation ceremonies for the men, which were always done in the 'haus tambaran' with a very tall, forward sloping front that was highly decorated with traditional emblems, and sometimes even with the skulls of their defeated tribal enemies.

Haus Tambaran

At Aitape we were able to visit a Christian mission leper colony, where basic medical supervision was provided. The poor people here were mainly missing one or more toes, and less commonly a finger. Their first knowledge that they had this disease would be when waking up on the sleeping mat on the floor of their village hut, they found that during the night a rat had chewed the toe off without even waking them up!

The mineral exploration conducted in this early stage of my career was very exciting. We would start collecting river sand samples close to the coast, specifically only particles finer than 80 mesh, which we obtained by using a stainless steel sieve. However, the larger rivers went far up into the mountains and there were very few places to land in a helicopter. The usual place was on the river itself, often on the outside of a major bend where the river bed was wider and there was a boulder strewn beach. So we would land slowly, balancing the helicopter's floats on the boulders.

Stream sediment sampling

Dropping down onto a river bed through a hole in the forest canopy with jungle vines dangling close to the tail rotor is a fairly hair-raising experience! My friend Dave Binney on Bougainville was a master at this.

While a helicopter can descend vertically, it cannot also take off vertically beyond the limit of the ground effect. We needed to have a rising flight path out. On several occasions we were overloaded, and had to leave rock samples behind. On other occasions we had to chop trees down to clear a flight path, almost skimming the tree tops as we flew out.

In the primary rain forest, for example in the Torricelli mountains, it was relatively easy to walk. The dense canopy killed off anything else from growing underneath.

But in the forest there were other hazards, including wild boars. While Bougainville only had pythons, mainland New Guinea also had deadly vipers, and on several occasions I narrowly missed stepping on one. Then there were the pig traps set by jungle villagers, often just a sapling bent over with a pegged noose at the end, or a pit covered with light branches. Then of course there were also the mosquitoes and the leaches. If we got a cut, we had to try to keep it dry. On several occasions I developed a tropical ulcer that went deep into my shin bone, necessitating me to stay at base until Neosporin antibiotic powder had healed the wound.

Our equipment consisted of a trace map of the rivers drawn from aerial photographs, a set of waterproof numbered paper sample bags, an 80 mesh sieve and collection pan, our geological pick and a waterproof notebook. We also had a little bottle of pH indicator liquid, so that we could measure the acidity of the river water at each sampling point. We wore an orange fluorescent over-shirt, and had rubber-soled canvas boots that had drain holes to let the water out because we spent a lot of time walking in the river itself. I would have an assistant, either from the ship or from a local village. I carried a marine emergency flare so that in the event of an accident like a broken leg, we could let off the flare when we heard the chopper searching for us above the forest canopy.

An interesting cult developed in Paua New Guinea, called the 'Cargo Cult'. The isolated villagers knew that the planes (balus) and helicopters (mixmaster bilong Jesus) they saw usually carried interesting goods, which they believed rightfully belonged to them.

So they would build big model planes on a long strip of cleared ground, to attract the next balus to come down and land on their pretend airstrip, a bit like wooden decoy ducks placed on a lake to attract wild ducks to fly down within reach of waiting shooters.

After our exploration of the north-east new Guinea coast the CRAE Star went down into the Solomon Islands, and explored most of the islands using the stream sediment sampling technique. A fair amount of time was spent exploring the island of Guadalcanal, a major focus of the war in the Pacific. There was war wreckage everywhere, and I used to have a picture of myself sitting astride the main gun of a Japanese destroyer that had been captured by the Americans who towed it into a coastal swamp at the east end of Guadalcanal and left it there.

One day when we were back at the wharf in Rabaul, a man came to repair the refrigeration system in the hold. He was doing some brazing of the pipes, which he had set up on the top of some drums placed on the rear deck. He was busy brazing away when our Ian Whitcher came up to him and asked cheerfully "Do you know what's in those drums?" The man's face turned white as he turned off his brazing gun. He was brazing on top of the 130 octane Avgas used to fuel the helicopter!

On occasion I would be given the ship's small outboard motor boat, a small aluminium dinghy, and with an Islander assistant I would go along the coast to gain entry to a selected river that we needed to do stream sediment sampling on. At the mouth of one river, the water was very shallow, and I stopped the motor and we rowed gently into the river mouth. Suddenly a huge tail went up in the air and there was a big splash as a crocodile moved off! We had rowed over the top of it!

Many of the coastal streams we had to sample were protected at the coast by a near impenetrable tangle of mangroves, which were difficult to clamber through and had very sharp roots sticking up through the mud. On top of this, they often carried thick clouds of mosquitoes, but so long as you had a machete and kept chopping, they couldn't land to bite you!

One day when we were working on Guadalcanal we landed at a central drop-off point and went off on foot to do our stream sediment sampling on several close-by rivers. When I had finished my particular river and got back, the others were already there at the starting point, and they could see me coming. To re-join the group I had to walk across a seemingly near-dry riverbed that had minimal water flowing. Off I stepped on to the river bed. Weighed down by my haversack of equipment and samples, to my horror I went straight down in a quicksand! I clung desperately to a small dead branch that was there, which allowed me to keep my head up! There was a big roar of laughter, and Ian said "Jeez, Mike, you finally got your arse wet!" Someone found a long branch which they poked out to me. I managed to grab it and they pulled me into the bank where I got out. Fortunately a little further up the river I found a pool of water and was able to rinse all the sand out of my clothes.

Ian did not have the last laugh however. A few days later when conducting a similar exercise, we had landed at a small village in the hope of buying some fresh vegetables before we went back to the ship. We bought some small round cucumber-like vegetables called chokos, and some beans. We got back into the helicopter and the pilot fired her up and we slowly rose above the ground, but there was very little lift due to the hot air close to ground. The pilot went to full pitch and maximum lift on his rotor blades, and still we were only hovering. Meanwhile we had drifted over some of the tall bean poles in the village garden, so could not go back to the ground because of the inevitable damage to the rotor blades. "Someone will have to get out" said the pilot. Ian was next to the door, and volunteered to get out. He lowered himself onto the chopper floats, and then dropped to the ground - up to his waist in a mud hole! With Ian's weight gone we were able to lift off and land again close by, unload our samples and vegetables, and then go back to pick Ian up.

We worked our way down to the east end of Guadalcanal, where there was a large stretch of open water called Marau Sound, protected from the open sea, and dotted with small islands. We anchored close to a Catholic mission station, and the priest and some of his helpers came out to the ship to have a meal with us. A few days later, we got caught in a typhoon that bore down on us with amazing speed. The pilot raced up to the chopper to lash it down so that it would not get blown overboard. The interface between the sea and the air above could not be seen, as the wind had whipped it into a foggy foam. During the night the ship dragged its anchor in the soft mud, and eventually the chain snapped. The ship was nearly blown onto some reefs at the edge of the shore. The engine was started and Charlie had to stay up all night and continuously steer to keep the ship from getting blown on to the reef.

The next day when the typhoon was gone, we could see the damage. Many flimsy native buildings on shore had been destroyed. The sea surface was littered with dead or dying seagulls and terns, many with broken wings. We were able to rescue an enormous male frigate bird that was still alive but too exhausted to fly. He rested for some time on our front deck and we gave him some fish to eat. After some hours of rest he was able to fly off slowly to a nearby frigate bird nesting colony. The loss of our heavy anchor needed to be remedied if possible. At the Catholic mission they had a compressor and one of the brothers could scuba dive. He came out to the ship with two scuba sets, and together we searched in the area where we believed the anchor had been lost, in about 70 feet of water. But the bottom of the sound was covered in thick soft mud, and we could find no trace either of the anchor or the missing section of chain.

Locally there was an Australian owner who had a copra plantation, selling the dried coconut meat from his palms. He also had a compressor and was a trained scuba diver. He had married a beautiful Polynesian girl with long black hair, and they had a little child. He had a magnificent collection of tropical sea shells, all collected alive while diving. By amazing good luck he had stumbled across an underwater breeding patch of a very rare cone shell, called Conus gloriamaris, or Glory of the Seas. At that time, one shell in mint condition was worth about USD 200. In those days marketing was the difficulty, and there were no laptop computers for on-line sales as there are today. Today the price for a shell in good condition is about USD 75.

Ian had a friend at Queensland University who was doing research on different species of tropical sand flies. Often while waiting for the chopper to come and pick us up on the beach at the mouth of a river we had been sampling, we would help Ian's entomologist friend by collecting sand flies. The technique was simple. We had little tubes with us full of ethyl alcohol. So we rolled up our shirt sleeve, and sure enough, after a few minutes one would be conscious of a burning sting administered by the tiny flying teeth! We would then put a drop of saliva on the end of our index finger, dab it onto the hungry sandfly, and lift him off our skin. It was then just a matter of uncorking the little tube of alcohol, and upending him into the alcohol. On the label we wrote the date, the approximate location, and whether it was bright sunshine, slightly cloudy or overcast, etc. All in the interests of science, of course!

On another occasion I took the outboard motor boat, and we went up the coast a little way past the surf which was crashing onto the coral barrier reef. We found an entrance and went into the lagoon, and then up a very narrow river to do some steam sediment sampling of the river and its tributaries. This river was not friendly, and close to the mouth there were a lot of fallen trees that bridged the river. Some we struggled to push the boat under, and sometimes we had to lift the boat over it. Then the river got a bit wider and we were able to motor along. Suddenly we hit a submerged log and lost power, although the motor was still running! I could rev the motor up and down, but we were going nowhere. Then I realised what had happened. The propeller was held on to the end of the drive shaft by a pin, which was sheared in half when we hit the log. A problem was immediately apparent - we had no spare locking pin!

We searched round desperately in the bottom of the boat, and found a nail that was about the right diameter. We got the boat going again and headed back, past the fallen logs. By the time we got back onto the beach, it was dusk. A wind had come up, and a heavy surf was crashing over the razor-sharp coral on the barrier reef. I was not game to look for the gap in the reef under those conditions, so we went back along the lagoon towards the ship. When we got back to the ship, it was dark. Rudi and Ian were cross with me for coming back so late, and thinking they would have to organise a search party for us the next day. But when I explained our mishaps, and the way we had successfully overcome them, they relaxed.

One day the CRAE Star was cruising just off a reef, looking for an entry through the outer reef into the lagoon that lay closer to shore. Archie had his British Admiralty charts of the islands, but they weren't totally accurate unfortunately. Based on his charts and the image on his radar screen, he thought he saw a gap and confidently signalled 'full speed ahead' to the crew in the engine room. The boys at the bow of the ship started to wave frantically, but it was too late, and we drove straight up onto the reef and came to a stop.

Masks and flippers were put on, and the crew inspected the hull. Fortunately no holes had been formed, but the propellor had lost a few blades. Some heavy anchor chains were taken out by small outboard boats and dropped, and we tried to winch ourselves off backwards. But we were stuck fast. It was realised that we would have to wait for a full high tide to get off. Meanwhile, our exploration work had to continue, so we geologists got into the chopper and off we went to do our stream sediment sampling. When we flew back to the ship in the late afternoon, the ship was nowhere to be seen!

A flat white sheet of mist hung over the coast. We went lower and lower, peering through the mist. Suddenly we could see the ship, and landed with the last teaspoon of fuel left in the chopper's tanks! The high tide came and we were able to slowly reverse off the reef. Then we limped into Gizo island where they had a wharf, and we were able to tie up. Fortunately we had a spare propellor, and the broken one was replaced.

I did not get to explore the island of Malaita with the rest of the team, and it was just as well. The Malaitans used to be fairly hostile to white people, and their track record already included spearing a few Christian missionaries to death. I heard later that the rest of the guys had a whole village of men waving spears and bows and arrows at them. They had to run for the chopper and wave frantically to the pilot to get the blades spinning. Fortunately they managed to escape without injury.

Many years later around 1998 I was in Melbourne and having dinner with a friend and his wife. The wife was the daughter of a Christian missionary who was also a surgeon, who had run a missionary hospital on the coast of Malaita. The wife had grown up on Malaita until she left to go to high school in Australia. Due to my interest in the magic practiced by South Sea Islanders, I asked her if she or her family had experienced anything which we westerners would consider to be magic. She said that she had, and told me this story. A young girl from a village up the coast was a patient at the mission hospital and was in a coma, kept alive on a drip. Eventually her father realised that he could do no more for this girl and sent a message to her parents in their village to come and see him. The parents came by canoe, and the surgeon explained that he could do no more medically for their daughter, and needed her bed for other patients. He gave them some drip to keep their daughter alive, and explained that he had already prayed often for Jesus to save her. The parents asked if it was alright if they prayed to their own Gods to help their daughter. "Of course" said the surgeon, and he lent them one of his hospital orderlies to help paddle the three hours journey back to their village, as the girl's mother had to cradle her while the men paddled. One and a half hours back into their journey, the girl came out of her coma and told her mother that she was very hungry!

In addition to my time on Bougainville, mainland PNG and the Solomons, I had a short assignment to some exploration going on in New Britain at a place called Uasilau, where the program was managed by Dave Mackenzie. The early target here was some copper and molybdenum-bearing laterites, and prospecting pits were dug and sampled. At this stage, no exploratory diamond drilling had been conducted. One of the young geologists in the Uasilau team had slipped while negotiating a waterfall, and had broken his arm. So I helped to keep the work going while his arm healed up.

I went back to Bougainville to resume my former duties. By this time most of the accommodation had moved from Barapena to Panguna Flat about 2 miles away, where we had a lot more locally built dongas with bamboo plaited walls, sac-sac sheets for roofing, and flap panels instead of windows.

Panguna Flat dongas

The locals living at Guava village upstream of the Panguna camp thought that we were stealing their land, and they started defecating in the river that flowed down from the high ridges past the Panguna camp. At that time we had only a very small water tank, and no chlorination or water filtration facilities. Our drinking water was pumped from the river. I got a persistent diarrhoea, and started taking an off-the-shelf traveller medication called Enterovioform. Initially I took one pill a day, but it didn't help, so I then took two a day, which also didn't help. I got up to taking eight pills a day, which was the maximum recommended. Still no improvement, and also I had noticed that my fingers and toes were starting to tingle. So I arranged for a chopper trip to the coast, and went to the Kieta base hospital where they gave me some other medicine that did work. Several years later, Enterovioform was withdrawn from sale. Enthusiastic pill poppers in Japan who had exceeded the dose were left permanently paralysed in wheel-chairs. The first symptom of the nerve damage they suffered was the tingling I had felt in my fingers!

We were at Panguna Flat one weekend, and I think it was a Sunday morning when everyone was relaxing. Suddenly a delegation of men arrived from Guava village higher up in the hills, and they walked into the centre of the camp. All had spears except for an old bow-legged man with a bow and some arrows, and some who had armfuls of grey things. They all banged the end of their spears into the ground. The old man with the bow said in a loud voice "Ol yu pella bilong CRA, luklukim long pawpaw e stop!" (All you people from CRA – take a look at the pawpaw tree!) We all looked at the fruit bearing pawpaw tree that was about 50 yards away. The old man drew his bow, and the biggest pawpaw fruit on the tree exploded as his arrow went through it. "All yu pella bilong CRA, RAUS!" This meant "Get the hell out of here now!" The men all banged their spears on the ground again, and then walked off, some of them depositing their armfuls of grey things onto a heap as they did so. When they had gone we inspected the grey things. The Guava villagers had gone up all our surveyed lines where we had done our soil augering, and pulled out all the concrete survey pegs.

In the Panguna Flat camp we had no firearms. Back at Barapena there was a detachment of ten PNG police led by a sergeant. The police had old WWII 303 rifles with blocked-up barrels, and the sergeant had an automatic shotgun. There was no telephone connection between Barapena and Panguna.

I used to sleep from then on with my window flaps bolted, and my door wedged shut. Just in case, I also loaded a compressed-air speargun that I had with me in my room, that I used for spearfishing when down on the coast.

Before leaving Bougainville, in addition to core logging I was involved with a survey of the igneous intrusions at the north end of the island. We also did stream sediment sampling up the east coast of Bougainville, travelling on a small cabin launch called 'Jennifer'. However, no positive indications of copper mineralisation were found in the samples we collected. One of the last diamond drill holes that I logged went horizontally into the base of the high-grade deposit at Panguna, to check out the rock types along the line of a proposed tunnel.

The 'Jennifer' launch.

On one of my annual leaves back to Melbourne in 1967, I was asked to go to the pub for a beer by Don Carruthers, which I did. He asked me how things were going up on site, and I mentioned that I had managed to get down to the coast when the Kieta Choral Festival was on. The Kieta Choral Festival was famous, and visitors would come from all over PNG to hear the singing, put on by the singers from the different Christian mission schools. There were Catholics, Presbyterians, Methodists, and also Seventh Day Adventists. Ken Phillips had a boat, and he would make it available for the drillers to go water skiing, also to their girlfriends who were often Australian nurses from the Nonga Base Hospital in Rabaul. I mentioned that some of the nurses had come over from Rabaul and immediately Don's attention quickened. How did they get over to Kieta, he asked. "On the regular commercial flight from Rabaul I suppose" I said. But Don was obviously suspicious. He checked the manifest of the flights put on by Green and Co., our supplies contractor who brought out our mail, fresh meat and other essential technical supplies every week. Just at the critical time of the festival, several of the cargo manifests said only "Fresh Meat!"

Shortly before I had left Bougainville I heard that Ken Phillips and Don Carruthers had had a furious row, and not long after that Ken had left the company! He joined Kennecott, the company exploring in mainland PNG that successfully discovered the massive Ok Tedi copper-gold deposit, subsequently acquired by BHP. Ken managed the completion of the exploratory development that led to the successful start up of the Ok Tedi mine. The Ok Tedi mine produces copper concentrate that also contains some gold, and the royalties still make a massive contribution to the PNG economy.

When I left Bougainville the weather was very bad, and dense cloud hung over Barapena and Panguna. There was a risk I would miss my plane to Rabaul, and my onward connections back to England. Helicopters need to have constant visual connection with the ground. But my friend Dave Binney took me up above the cloud, and got me safely to the coast to catch my plane.

Some years later I was attending a technical talk in Perth about the development of the Ok Tedi copper mine in mainland New Guinea, given by their MD at that time, Irwin Newman. In his presentation he included a shot of a place in the mountains close to the deposit which they now called Mount Binney, at the edge of a major steep scarp. Dave was then working at Ok Tedi, and had a geologist and a field assistant with him in the chopper when they got sucked into the scarp wall by a fierce down draft. The geologist got a broken arm, the field assistant was unhurt, and tragically Dave Binney was killed. He left his lovely wife and two daughters, and never got to realise his dream of retiring to farm black Aberdeen Angus cattle back in Scotland.

The famous open-pit copper mine at Panguna did not actually start production until 1972. A huge influx of workers was brought in from other parts of PNG, with representatives from many different tribes. A residential town was set up at Arawa, where previously there had only been a copra plantation. This understandably was all a severe culture shock for the local Bougainvilleans. To make matters worse, all the production royalties from the copper concentrate production went to the PNG government in Port Moresby, but little if any of it came back to Bougainville for local infrastructure and social facilities. Eventually a civil war broke out and the mine had to be abandoned in May 1989, but that is another story.

On 29th April 2020, Ken Phillips left this world, leaving his wife and two sons. He is mourned by all who knew him, and the whole economy of Papua New Guinea is still reaping his legacy to this day.

Ken Phillips alighting from helicopter

9

# MORE STUDY

After working for several years continuously in the tropics, in mainly jungle settings, I was beginning to wonder if the whole of the rest of my career was going to be like this. What can I do, I thought, that still involves rocks and minerals, but is much closer to civilisation? The answer was fairly obvious. I needed to go back to college and get some qualifications in Mineral Processing.

By now it was 1967, and I was just finishing two years of work with CRA as a Field Geologist. I made enquiries and was offered a scholarship to do an M.Sc. degree in Mineral Process Design, back at the Royal School of Mines in London. I had been away from my UK relatives for two years, and it was an opportunity too good to miss.

So back in Melbourne, I caught an Italian ship called the FairSky, which took me to Sydney, Tahiti, the Panama Canal, the island of Curacao, Lisbon and finally to Southampton, just north of my birthplace on the Isle of Wight.

The trip itself was both interesting and also an ordeal. The weather ranged from poor to horrible for the whole six-week journey. On the open ocean it was sometimes so rough that our plates of food on the dining room table would slide off onto the floor. People were sick all over the stair wells to the lower decks. Due to the closed air conditioning system, a virus went all round the ship, and at Lisbon someone had to be helicoptered off to go to hospital. I myself was sick for about three days, and spent most of that time in bed.

I made friends with a group of young adults and we partied and did our best to have fun. All kinds of Peyton Place dramas took place. At the entrance to the laundry drying room on D Deck where I had my single cabin, a woman posted a note saying "Would the person who stole my pink silk knickers please return them to the drying room?"

But the one that really grabbed me was the man whose heartfelt notice was left on a prominent notice board for all to read, "Would the man who has stolen my wife please note that although I have fed her and cared for her for the last thirty years, from now on I am assuming that YOU have taken over this duty!"

Despite the fact that our port stops were spoilt by rainy weather, I enjoyed the Tahitian dancing displays, the wild west atmosphere in Panama where the cops had their gun belt slung low, the shopping in Curacao, and the monuments in Lisbon to the Portuguese ocean explorers.

My mother came down from London to meet me off the ship at Southampton, and we drove home to Guibal Road in her car. So began a very intensive year of non-stop study, rewarded by my achieving an M.Sc. pass with distinction. I then managed to get a job offer to join the mineralogy and petrology group at AMDEL, a mineral research organisation in Adelaide, South Australia. I applied for immigration to Australia, and was interviewed at Australia House on the Strand in London. "What's the hurry" I was asked. "Are you running away from the police?" I explained that I had my new qualification, but no money, and was sponging off my widowed mother. I needed to get to Adelaide to start earning. My explanation was accepted, and for the fair exchange of GBP 10, I was given a migrant visa and a flight ticket to Adelaide in South Australia.

10

# Australia Again, and Mount Isa

In November 1968 I arrived in Adelaide as a "Ten Pound Pom", an English person or "Pommie" who had managed to migrate to Australia by simply paying a ten pound fee. The descendants of the original British settlers who had come to Australia were not very welcoming, and there were frequent references to "Pommies" and commonly to "Pommie Bastards" as well.

My new employer was a group called AMDEL, a joint venture between the South Australian government and private interests. AMDEL was an acronym for Australian Mineral Development Laboratories. My new job was as a Scientific Officer assigned to the Mineralogy and Petrology section at Frewville, one of the Adelaide suburbs. So my new duties consisted mainly of looking at thin sections of all kinds of rocks (igneous, metamorphic or sedimentary), and then assigning them an appropriate rock type identity and preparing an appropriate descriptive report.

I found myself a small flat in North Plympton, and bought a new car on hire purchase, a cream-coloured Holden Torana. As a keen rugby player, I signed up with the North Adelaide amateur rugby club, and played in weekend matches during the winter season.

I became aware after some months that AMDEL also had another laboratory, where all the mineral processing testwork investigations were done. This laboratory was in a suburb called Thebarton, and was close to Port Adelaide. I pointed out that I now had an M.Sc. degree in Mineral Process Design, and expressed an interest in getting a transfer to Thebarton. In due course this was arranged, and in addition at Thebarton I acquired the role of on-site mineralogist, providing quick mineralogical feedback to the metallurgists running the many various projects that the Thebarton laboratory was engaged in.

At both Frewville and Thebarton I met other geologists and metallurgists who became lifelong friends, with whom I am still in touch today, although they are now mostly living in other Australian states. I also maintained my hobby of scuba diving and underwater photography. Christies Beach south of Adelaide was a favourite spot, as there was quite a long jetty there with a ladder at the end, by which you could descend onto a flat-topped reef that was just under water at high tide. The reef was covered with a lot of weed and there were many fish in attendance, including Leather Jackets, Old Wives, and Sweep. Generally the water was clear, and I got a lot of good shots with my Nikonos underwater camera. The shallow cliffs at Christies Beach consisted of calcareous marls containing quite a few fossils, and I still have a shark's tooth fossil that I dug out of the cliffs there.

As a young man who had escaped from a life in tropical jungles, I now turned my attention to meeting young ladies, and after about one year of dating with Raelene, we got married in June 1970 at the Black Forest Methodist Church, and moved into a new flat. Raelene had a job as the Secretary for a company called Mining Supplies. When we first met, Raelene lived with her Mum and Dad and two brothers, Glen and Raymond, and I got to know them all well.

A few months after our marriage, I became aware of a better job opportunity at the mining town of Mount Isa, in north-west Queensland. I applied and got the job as Research Metallurgist attached to the lead-zinc concentrator, and we moved there in

November 1970. We were at Mt Isa for more than four years, and had friends there with whom I am still in touch.

Our stay in Mt Isa was marred by a terrible thing from which my wife Raelene never fully recovered.

She was pregnant and we were expecting our first child. Rae asked her doctor if she could play squash, and incredibly he said "Yes, if you play gently". (It is impossible to play squash gently, unless you play by yourself). All was going well until she played squash again. Around midnight her waters broke, and I rushed her to the Mount Isa base hospital where the next morning she delivered two little daughters, one still-born. The other, who we named Louise Elizabeth, survived only a few hours, but Rae was able to hold her briefly in her arms. They were 13 weeks premature, and the facilities for premature babies in Mt Isa at that time were minimal. Louise and her sister were buried together in the same coffin box at the Mount Isa Cemetery.

Later when we had moved to Bunbury in Western Australia, our attempts at making a family went better, and in 1975 our eldest son Alexander was born. Later when we were living in Whyalla, South Australia our second son Lincoln was born. However, I think the loss of our two daughters weighed heavily on Rae, and contributed to her depression that kicked in before our marriage finally broke up in 1990.

I wish that I had been able to comfort her with some words spoken by Sai Baba, that children who are still-born are advanced souls who need minimal time on the earth plane to fulfil their karmic debt. But in 1990, I still didn't know who Sai Baba was.

# 11

# MINERAL SANDS

In late 1974 I resigned from Mt Isa in response to being side-lined by my boss, but took the prior precaution of getting accepted for another position on the other side of Australia.

My new position was as Mineral Research Engineer for Western Titanium Ltd who had their operations based on a very rich heavy mineral sands deposit at Capel, a little village south of the town of Bunbury in Western Australia. My new boss Mike Davies had previously been the Mill Superintendent at the Mt Isa Pb-Zn Plant. In addition he was an alumni of my university college back in London.

Raelene was pregnant, so she did not come with me as I drove down to her parents' house in Adelaide. Rae came down by plane and we rested for a couple of days with Rae's parents. I then took off again, driving westwards from Adelaide, across the vast Nullarbor Plain and into Western Australia where I stayed at a border motel. Then it was on to Kalgoorlie, through Northam, down to Perth and on to Bunbury, where I stayed in a hotel for the night. On that last day's drive to Bunbury, there was torrential rain and incredibly strong winds. I had an aluminium dinghy clamped to the roof rack, and several times the wind nearly blew me off the road. A rental house had been lined up for us in Bunbury, and once I had checked it out I let Rae know and she flew over to Perth. I met her at the airport, and brought her down to our new home.

Bunbury was a pleasant little town with excellent beaches and a lighthouse placed close to the harbour entrance. To get to the beach we just had to walk a few hundred yards up our street, over a sand dune ridge and we were down at the beach. Further south there were some excellent scuba diving spots, and crayfish became a regular part of our diet, along with Blue Manna crabs. From time to time I was able to spear a good-sized fish for our table too. For a long time I had wanted to take up karate, and in Bunbury I finally was able to join the local club, and kept fit by regular running.

The day for the birth of our child came and Rae was well looked after in the St John of God hospital in Bunbury, where Alexander was born on 5th January 1975.

After about a year we moved down to Capel itself, where the company had built some new bungalows. Our house was now only five minutes away from work, and avoided the somewhat dangerous drive from Bunbury to Capel. The main driving hazard was the kangaroos, that either early in the morning or at dusk were magnetically attracted to a car's headlights. Their favourite trick was to wait by the side of the road, and then leap out in front of you at the last moment.

If you hit a big 'roo it would demolish the front of your car, so we would slow down if we could see their eyes shining at us in the headlights.

Getting back and front lawns to grow on barren yellow sand at our Capel house took a fair bit of effort, but before too long we had both lawns and some flower beds. Beautiful green Kangaroo paws grew abundantly in the local scrub, and I transplanted a few to our flower beds. Around Christmas time the golden flowers of the native W.A. Christmas Tree would come into bloom. Although it looked like an ordinary tree it is actually a parasite, and grows on decayed branches below the ground surface.

Western Australia is blessed with a wonderful array of beautiful wild flowers, that come out in spring in the scrub and in the forests, and in the northern desert areas too. In our back garden we would often see big spider-hunting wasps. They would sting and anaesthetize a spider, place it in their mud nest cell, then lay their egg on it. When the egg hatched the wasp grub would feed on the spider.

We made good friends in our new company housing enclave. After about two years with Western Titanium, I was offered a PhD scholarship back at my college in London. Western Titanium agreed to let me take samples from their various deposits to be used for my research, which was to be on the minerals present in the heavy mineral sands. It was an opportunity to introduce Rae and Alex to all my UK relatives. My mother had offered to let us stay at her place and just pay for our food and electricity. So in September 1976 we placed all our furniture in store, and I booked our flight tickets to London. A wise precaution that I took before we left was to obtain Australian nationality. As a British-born resident I could only be away from Australia for a maximum of three years, and of course there was no way that I could confidently predict that I would have my PhD within that time. So I applied, paid a fee of about twenty dollars, and visited an Immigration Department official who got me to swear an Oath of Allegiance to Her Majesty the Queen of Australia. It was as simple as that.

I found this all highly amusing as in Britain where I was born, I had never had to do this. Our allegiance to Her Majesty the Queen was just taken for granted.

# 12

# YET MORE STUDY - PILED HIGHER AND DEEPER

While previously living in both Mt Isa and in Capel, my mother Joan had come out from Melbourne to spend a holiday with us, and both she and my wife Rae seemed to get on fairly well. But It did not go so well in our next attempt to live together.

Initially everything was fine, but my mother had changed since we were last together. She had completed a course in Montessori teaching of children, and had a job as an Assistant Teacher at a Montessori School. Their prevailing mantra was that children should never be physically disciplined when they were naughty, as anything like smacking would severely cramp and inhibit their natural creativity.

Rae and Alex would be at home for most of the day, while I drove off to college early in the morning, and returned later in the evening. I was amazed at the way Joan now treated our son Alex. When he was sitting on the lounge, we made him sit nicely with his feet out. But when Joan was there she ignored all this and encouraged him to jump up and down using the lounge like a trampoline! Uncle Russell came over one day, and his eyes went wide as saucers when he saw Alex jumping up and down on the lounge. "I know what you're thinking", I thought, as his own children had never been allowed to do this when they visited Joan's house.

One night Alex was particularly naughty. We had put him to bed upstairs, and about half an hour later he came down into the lounge room again. So I took him back to bed, and he seemed to settle down. I tip-toed downstairs again and I think we were watching the news on television when he came down again. Once again I took him back to bed, but again and again he came down again. Finally after about nine tries, I spoke to him again, and said that if he got out of bed and came down once more, I was going to smack him. I then took him back to bed. My mother Joan had witnessed and heard the whole cycle, but had said nothing.

Unbelievably, about ten minutes later, Alex again got out of bed and came down into the lounge area again. True to my word, I smacked him once on his bottom, and he cried. I then took him back to bed. When I came down again, Joan exploded and started a big row with myself and Rae. "You both have filthy vile tempers" she fumed, "You're not fit to be parents".

A few days later we had a planned family visit to see Russell and Barbara at their home in Leighton Buzzard in Bedfordshire. Joan sat in the back of the car and glowered at us the whole way. When we arrived she went with Russell into his study and in a loud voice that could be heard all over their house, she repeated the same claim she had made to us directly, that we had filthy vile tempers, were not fit to be parents etc., etc. Once we were back at her house in Lee, she repeated the same thing to our neighbours, and rang up everyone on her side of the family to tell them the same thing.

My Aunt Gwen however, and relatives on my father's side of the family continued to treat us normally, but the rest of Joan's side of the family displayed a very frosty stance from then on. Rae and I tried to not get upset, and continued to be as civil as we could to Joan, but whatever opinion we expressed about the weather or the news, Joan would immediately tell us that we were wrong. I found all this very stressful, and often Rae would take Alex out in his pram just to get away from her. I started developing ulcer symptoms. So I started to avoid speaking to Joan unless I had to, and Rae did the same. It saved us getting into more arguments. Joan then told all her relatives and the neighbours that we were ignoring her in her own house.

One night when I was in the lounge and playing some classical music, Joan went beserk again. "If I'm so terrible to live with" she said, "why don't you go and live somewhere else?. But of course, you will never do that because it would hurt your pocket!"

Being on a small student grant we were already spending a lot of the money left in our Australian savings. But enough was enough. When Rae came back later from visiting a friend, I told her what had happened, and we agreed that we would leave.

I made enquiries and found a small flat that was close enough to college and that we should just be available to afford until my Piled Higher and Deeper (PhD) was finished. We packed up our stuff and moved out. I left a note for Joan saying that we had accepted her invitation to leave, and gave her my contact details at the college.

The peace and relief of being in our own flat where Joan couldn't bother us was enormous. Rae's whole demeanour picked up. My ulcer symptoms disappeared. I got re-stuck into my PhD research with enthusiasm. The final interview with the adjudicating examiner came and went, and I was awarded my PhD in January 1980.

Along with working to achieve this satisfactory outcome, I had been approaching many companies for a job back in Australia. Finally I had a win with BHP, and I submitted to their medical tests as arranged by their London representative. I was given a job at their Central Research Laboratory in Newcastle, NSW, and our flights were booked. We arranged for our stuff to be shipped back to Australia, and I arranged a final visit to Joan to say goodbye as we were now going back to Australia.

I drove over to her house. And we then had a conversation in the lounge. "Don't think that I'm going to leave you anything in my will" she began, "because I would rather leave it to the Cats' and Dogs' Home. You had better choose what you want from your father's book-case!" Certain books and paintings that I would have liked to have had were apparently already earmarked for other relatives, so I chose some of the books, including a book that had belonged to my grandfather, called Foxe's Book of Martyrs. I said goodbye and left.

# 13

# BHP Newcastle and Whyalla

We arrived in Newcastle and found a rented flat. First job was to buy a mattress as we couldn't afford to buy a bed as well. I settled into my new job and got to know my new colleagues. A school was picked out for Alex, and we settled into the Newcastle life-style. Nice beaches were close, also forest reserves and an attractive coastline, I took up karate again and used to keep fit by running along Dudley Beach at the weekends.

Dudley beach was not all that popular, being well south from Newcastle so less people bothered to go there. But it was more than a mile long with cliffs at both ends and no houses nearby. I discovered that the north end was also a nudist beach too. One day I was running towards the north end when I saw a woman about to go into the water for a swim, and as I got closer I realised with amazement that she had no bathers on! She saw my eyes as wide as saucers as I ran past, and skipped off into the waves with a laugh.

We found a nice little house in a suburb called Rankin Park, and I approached my bank to get a loan. The local branch manager went through my customer file. "When you left for England in 1976, you didn't accept our quote for your family's air tickets", he began. I explained that the travel agency round the corner from their Bunbury Branch on the other side of Australia had offered me the same thing for three hundred dollars cheaper, and asked him what choice he would have made! After our stay in UK our savings were very low, so the first task was to find some money. I cashed in my life assurance savings, and we had enough for the deposit. We moved into our new little house and settled into the area. The semi-tropical climate meant there were plenty of mosquitoes around, and at night we could hear them buzzing against the fly-wire security screen of our open back door as they tried to get in. Our closeness to the Hunter River caused us some problems too, due to the presence of huge mosquitoes called 'Hexham Greys'. Worse, our son Alex collected a few bites from time to time, and was obviously allergic to them as he would come up in a large lump as big as a five cent coin.

The BHP Central Research Laboratory where I worked focussed mainly on testing of the many different types of coals present in the New South Wales coalfields, so I learnt the basics of coal deposit testing and evaluation, and also got involved with their research on manganese ores and the sintering of iron ore fines. At that time BHP had some big iron ore blast furnaces in Newcastle which in turn fed pig iron to their steel works. The unions in Newcastle were very strong. On the wharf, the Maritime Workers Union had systemic overmanning. On night shift, the operators used to take turns to sleep the whole shift on their camp beds. BHP was trying to put a stop to these kinds of practice, and eventually succeeded, but at just the wrong time for us.

I became aware that BHP had another laboratory at Whyalla in South Australia, which serviced their South Australian iron ore mines and the steelworks at the Whyalla Port. But the Whyalla laboratory was very different in one way, in that although heavily involved with iron ore testing it did no work with coal. Instead it did testwork for BHP's other mines for commodities including copper, tin and gold. A vacancy developed there for a metallurgist to manage the Whyalla laboratory. I put my hand up and was awarded the position. So BHP moved us and all our family effects, including our car to Whyalla, where we were given a nice house in Bean Street for the very reasonable rent of $15 per week.

Whyalla lies on the western side of St Vincent's Gulf, and in earlier years had also had a ship building industry as well as the blast furnace and steel works. The surrounding countryside is very arid, and in summer the temperature regularly rises higher than 40° C. Prickly pear cactus grows well here, almost like a weed. But in winter when South Australia's capital city Adelaide is cold and drowning in rain, Whyalla often remains bright and sunny. Our back garden was a joy as it had many fruits, including Lady Finger grapes, oranges, lemons and even some cumquats.

At this time, Rae's parents were still alive in Adelaide, and it was only a four and a half hour drive for us to get over there to see them together with her two brothers, Raymond and Glen.

In 1981 we had a new addition to our family, and Lincoln was born in the Whyalla Hospital. Meanwhile Alex attended the local primary school.

Our house was a five minute drive from the laboratory which sat in the shadow of the blast furnace, and also was very close to the coke ovens that produced coke for the blast furnace. One of the gases that can escape from the roof of the coke ovens is carbon monoxide, and in 1981 instruments for measuring carbon monoxide levels were not readily available. So when maintenance workers had to check various things on the roof of the coke ovens, they would take with them a canary that came from a little aviary close by. The canary was carried in a little cage, and if the canary fell off his perch, it was a warning for the maintenance crew to come down as fast as they could.

One day late in our stay at Whyalla, someone deliberately opened the aviary door, and all the canaries escaped. Whoever thought that they were getting back at the company, they didn't do the canaries any favours. As escaped cage birds, they would either starve to death or be pecked to death by the other local birds.

One of the interesting characters at the main BHP Whyalla store was the expediter. He would order all the spare parts needed by the different sections of the Whyalla operations. He could talk on two phones at once, one stuck in the crook between his cheek and his shoulder, and one in his hand.

One day when I went to the store to get a new pair of safety boots, only the expediter was there. He signalled to me that I needed to wait while he finished off some business. He was talking to a supplier in Adelaide, whose goods had not arrived on time in Whyalla. "Can you hear me well?" asked the expediter. I could hear the man in Adelaide gulp, as he replied "Yes". "Well then"" said the expediter, "You have two choices! Either those goods are here on my desk tomorrow morning at 9 am, or I'll jump into my car and come down to Adelaide and cut your nuts off with a rusty penknife! Do you understand?" Again I heard the man gulp as he said "Yes"!

The unions were entrenched in Whyalla as well as in Newcastle. A lot of goods would mysteriously disappear from the Whyalla store, and their theft was often not discovered until one of the periodic audits. One enterprising person who was scheduled to be laid off in a few months came up with a brilliant plan. He ordered stainless steel sheet, axle shafts, wheels and tyres etc and during company time made himself a magnificent stainless steel trailer.

Just before he was due to leave anyway, he now had the problem of having to go through the security gate to get it off site. He and his mates came up with another successful plan. So he hooked it up to his car and started spray painting it with the company spray gun and some paint from the store. Meanwhile his buddy rang security and said "Hey, there's some guy using company paint to spray his trailer. If you go now to the car park you'll catch him doing it!" Sure enough, the security jeep pulls up and out steps the security guard. "What the hell do you think you're doing? Get that trailer off site now!", and the guard promptly escorted him out to the security gate. Some months later when a check was done to find who ordered the stainless steel, the clever gentleman had disappeared and was no longer living in Whyalla.

When we left Newcastle, we rented out our house in Rankin Park, and continued paying the mortgage. But the rent received did not completely cover the mortgage so we decided to sell the house. Just then BHP finalised a deal with the Newcastle Unions, who wanted a guaranteed 40-hour week. BHP agreed to the forty hour week in return for an end to over-manning. Thousands of workers were laid off in Newcastle, and suddenly there were thousands of houses up for sale. Property values plummeted, and we sold at a loss.

While running the metallurgical laboratory in Whyalla, I received a promotion to Senior Staff. This was like finally being recognised as a human being whose recommendations were to be considered carefully, rather than being a worker whose only function was to do as he was told. The new status included being invited to the Senior Staff Christmas Party, along with your wife. The Commodore of the BHP fleet owned some oyster leases in Coffin Bay near Port Lincoln, south of Whyalla. The menu offered a choice of half a dozen or a full dozen. Having always liked fresh oysters, I ordered a dozen, but quickly wished that I hadn't. The Coffin Bay oysters were huge, about four inches long and two inches wide! Having eaten them I had great difficulty eating all of the main meal.

While in Whyalla we needed another bed while Raelene was nursing our new baby son Lincoln, and I purchased an old brass bed from my neighbour, one of the technical superintendents at the Whyalla Plant. One night as I lay sleeping in it, I woke up in the night and could see a tall grey swirling shape at the end of the bed. I wondered if it was a ghost, and forced myself out of my drowsiness to focus on it more closely, whereupon it immediately vanished! The next time I saw my neighbour I asked him if the bed I had bought had a ghost associated with it. "Of course" said he. "Didn't I tell you about it?"

All good things must come to an end they say, and so it was in Whyalla. As part of the new forty hour week deal, BHP's Whyalla operations were also affected. One of the site managers was given the new job of hatchet-man. He went round the managers and superintendents one by one, and gave them their retirement package options. He came to the laboratory, and asked me what percentage of the laboratory's work was for the site iron ore operations, and what percentage was for other off-site BHP activities. I took this to mean that I also was likely to be lopped. Fortunately an opportunity came up back in Perth, as Chief of the Mines Department's Engineering Chemistry Laboratory. So back we came to Perth, in November 1982.

# 14

# Perth and Beyond

Back in Perth we rented a small house, while I settled into my new job which was based at a well-equipped laboratory in the suburb of Bentley. In this job I was a public servant, and so had access to a public service pension. The catch was that I had to join the Public Service Union, so I became a unionist for the first and only time in my life. I was in charge of a team of 18 staff. The work was quite varied, and mainly covered investigations on West Australian mineral deposits which meant iron ores, heavy mineral sands, coal, bauxites, graphite, gold, nickel and so on. Coming to Perth from Whyalla, we found the climate very unpleasant at first because of the humidity. Although Whyalla used to get hotter in summer than Perth, in Whyalla the air was very dry while in Perth it was noticeably much more humid.

We looked around for a house, and again I visited the local branch of my bank which in late 1982 was at the Bentley shopping centre. "Yes Mike" said the manager, "I can give you a loan, but I will expect you to give us all your insurance business, for your car, your house and the contents and so on". Having previously been conditioned by my experiences with the same bank in Bunbury and again in Newcastle, I stood my ground. "I'm quite happy with my existing insurance providers" I said, and "I really don't want to change. So either you agree to give me a mortgage, or if not, I will go to another bank that will!"

I put my bid in on the house we wanted which had a deadline for confirmation of the mortgage finance. As the date on which my bid expired approached, the property agent got nervous and told me that the bank was never going to give me the loan in time to meet the expiry at 2pm on a particular day. The day arrived and at 1.30 pm I received a call from the bank saying that the mortgage had been confirmed. I then had to drive like a bat out of hell to the bank, collect the letter and drive back to the property agent where I arrived five minutes before my bid expired.

Our new house was on a long narrow, block, with a very wide frontage and a lot of front lawn to cut. In the back garden we had a small swimming pool at one end and a tall Blue Gum tree at the other, that sucked so much moisture from the sandy soil that the grass refused to grow there.

Along the long back fence we had a narrow aviary, barely three feet wide. A small section near the swimming pool held canaries and some little quail. The rest of the aviary held about half a dozen budgerigars, who used to feed from a seed container placed against the back fence at the left hand end. Due to the birds' habit of dropping seed everywhere, we soon had a community of mice as well, and they became very ingenious about the way they managed to get access to more seed than the grains that fell to the ground. On several occasions I found mice sitting in the seed container's feeding tray, and set out to find out how they managed to get there. As soon as the mice saw me, they would always jump off and run away to their nearest hole in the aviary floor. Some ivy grew along the top of the fence, and had slightly extended into the fine chicken wire mesh that formed the roof of the aviary. It also extended down the fence until it nearly reached the aviary floor. So I hid with a pair of binoculars, and saw that they jumped onto the ivy and climbed up to the top of the fence. They then wriggled up through a hole in the chicken wire and ran along the top of the aviary and then wriggled through another hole to drop onto the seedbox tray.

So I cut back the ivy until it was too high for them to reach by jumping. But only a few days later, the mice were back in the seed tray. So again I hid and watched through binoculars. On the outside of the aviary close to the entry gate, a water cup was placed. This time the mice climbed up to the water cup and then jumped across the width of the aviary to land on the seed tray. So I moved the water cup so that it was too far away from the seed container. But sure enough, a few days later the mice were back in the feed tray. This time they climbed all the way up the chicken wire to reach the roof, on to the top, and then dropped through a hole onto the feed tray. So I put a sheet of thin plywood across the top of the cage so that they could no longer wriggle through a hole. This seemed to stop them for a while, but again they managed to get onto the feed tray. So, full of admiration for their ingenuity, I decided to leave them in peace.

In 1987 an interesting job became available in India, as part of a consulting project won by Robertson Research, who opened a Perth office although their head office remained in Sydney. We had a multidisciplined team including their MD, Ron Butler, a couple of mining engineers, two resource geologists and myself as metallurgist. The project was based in Bihar in eastern India, and we got there generally by flying first to Bombay and then to Calcutta. However on my first trip to join the team, I went in via Madras, then on to Calcutta. While in Singapore I contracted the flu, and by the time I arrived at Dumdum, the Calcutta airport, I was nearly exhausted. No one was there at the airport to meet me. I had a list of contact phone numbers, and began to ring them, one by one, but could not get an answer from any of them. Finally on my third iteration of ringing them all, I got through to someone. He explained that I had arrived in the middle of a religious holiday, and that it would take him two hours to come to the airport, so it would be better for me to take a taxi and come in. In addition to my luggage I had with me an $8000 Compac computer, one of the first portable units. Stepping outside the terminal I was surrounded by young boys who tried to take my luggage to their particular favourite taxi. Seeing my difficulty a policeman, who was dressed in khaki like a soldier, came to help me. He understood some English, so he told the Bengali driver where I wanted to go. I sat in the back and was alarmed by the torn upholstery and the fact that there was no fare meter. We started off on the trip into Calcutta through what seemed to be a very rough area. Huge rectangular pits (called tanks in India) had been dug on each side of the road and they were full of slimy green water. Some huge concrete sewer pipes were at the side of the road, and had families living in them. This didn't seem to be the main road from the airport to the city, and I became alarmed, thinking that the driver was taking me to some outer suburb. My passport would be stolen along with my Compac computer, my luggage would disappear, and my body would never be found!

But despite the foreboding appearances, it was indeed the main road to Calcutta. As we drove along, I saw a conical hill in the distance. The hill grew bigger as we got closer and I could see tiny things moving on the surface. Finally as we drove past I realised that it was an enormous rubbish dump, and the things moving on the surface were poor people scavenging for glass and reusable plastics.

Coming into Calcutta, the capital of Bengal, we had to cross over the Hooghly river, using the Howrah bridge. The bridge had been erected by the British Army during WWII. The day I was there, the bridge had a very mixed traffic, including overloaded trucks, a man walking with about six armchairs on his head, men running along pulling customers in their rickshaws, and a cow pulling a load of hay. In the late afternoon with the dust laden air, black smoky exhausts of trucks, pierced by occasional shafts of sunlight through the beams of the bridge, I thought I had come to Hades, the very gates of hell! Once over the Howrah bridge however, the roads and the buildings improved. I saw a sign in English for a big museum, and got the driver to stop. I went in and found a museum officer, a sari-clad lady who could speak perfect English, and asked her how to get to my target address, the Hindustan Copper Guest House. "Oh, it's just very close" she said, and started to give me directions. I persuaded her to come and tell the taxi driver in Bengali, who now clearly understood exactly where he had to go. Five minutes later we arrived, and I paid the taxi driver. The guest house manager came out and helped me bring my luggage and the computer in. "Fine!" he said, as he gave me a cup of tea. "Finish your tea and I will take you to the station to catch your train!" I protested that I was now totally exhausted and needed to stay the night to recover, and fortunately he agreed. So I did the six hour train trip the next day from Howrah to the station at Ghatsila on the Jamshedpur line, and caught a local taxi in to the Mosaboni copper mine where we were based.

In 1989 the term FIFO had not been invented, but our contract certainly required us to fly in and then fly out, only to fly back again later. We would spend seven or eight weeks on site, and then have about a two week break back in Australia, before flying back for another stint. At the mine, no telephone link with Calcutta was available. While on site I would write home, but no letters back from Rae ever arrived. Back on break she would insist that she had written. Eventually I complained to the post office about the missing mail that never reached me in India, and they did a check but found nothing. Towards the end of my contract, Rae admitted that she had not actually written back to me. "I prefer it when you're away', she said.

India is a very beautiful country, and in the two years I was there I saw every stage of the rice production from planting the seedlings, thinning them out, reaping with hand sickles, drying the stacked rice, threshing and then winnowing. Also I managed to see quite a lot of Indian classical dance, for which there are seven completely different systems. I managed to attend a wonderful presentation at a beautiful theatre in Calcutta. The presentation went for two full days and included examples of all the major styles. The title of the show was "The connection between Indian Classical Dance and Karate" so I simply could not resist attending. My favourite style was Mohiniyattam, the style from Kerala. The link between karate and their dances was immediately obvious, because many of the stances used by the dancers are exactly the same as the ones I had learnt for karate! I was also blown away by Kathak, from northern India, the original source of the dance style taken by Indian gypsies from Rajasthan across Europe to Spain where today it flowers as the spectacular styles of dancing known as Flamenco. From Manipur I also saw the Manipuri style, using stick fighting movements using the straight wooden poles known as Bo in Japan. This exposure convinced me beyond doubt, that karate originated in India. It was taken by Buddhist monks into China, where they taught the Chinese monks the basics of unarmed combat[1], where it morphed into Kung Fu. Then with social interaction between China and what is now known as Okinawa, the unarmed combat techniques were further developed by the Okinawans in secret at night in blacked-out houses, as only the Japanese Samurai were allowed to carry swords. So different styles developed in different Okinawan cities, Finally in 1928, Gichin Funakoshi, the leader of the Shotokan style went to Tokyo and gave a demonstration to the Japanese Emperor, in which he defeated the Emperor's personal body guards using unarmed combat. Karate was then taken up by the Japanese universities, and again by American troops in occupation after Japan was defeated. The troops took karate back to America, where it became popular, and the rest is history.

The poverty I saw in India was completely gut-wrenching, and it was very easy to see in Calcutta. At the dance festival I attended, in the interval after a performance I would be in the theatre foyer surrounded by more stunningly beautiful women than I have ever seen before together in one room. I spoke to an Indian gentleman and said to him "this theatre is as good or better as anything we have in Perth, yet outside in the street there are beggars dying, and lepers having their sores treated by nuns from Mother Teresa's convent.

---

[1] Karate's History and Traditions by Bruce A. Haines, Charles E. Tuttle Company, 1968.

How do you reconcile this opulence inside the theatre with the poverty outside?" The guy shrugged and said "We don't see it any more. We just step over it!"

A wonderful story about Calcutta was written by Dominic Lapierre[2], called the 'City of Joy', and it was later made into a film. I was told about this book by my boss, Ron Butler. I got a copy and tried to read it. Frequently I had to shut the book and put it away, as my eyes would fill with tears. However, I did finish it eventually. The film had been sanitised to a significant extent to make it less gut-wrenching than the book, as I found when I later watched it.

Having re-settled in Perth, I hoped that no more inter-state moves would be required. But it was not to be. After my marriage to Raelene broke up after twenty years in 1990, I married Alicia and ended up in Sydney NSW in 1994, but the marriage was a disaster and very short lived. I then moved to Melbourne in Victoria in 1996, then back to Perth in 2000. In 2006 I remarried to Tegshee, a Mongolian woman whom I met in August 2004 at Oyu Tolgoi, a new copper-gold mine in Mongolia. In 2007 our son William was born. We moved to Mt Isa in north-west Queensland in 2013.

In June 2016 we were coming back to Perth on holiday. We drove back from Mt Isa along an inland route that took us a total of six days, and we would spend each night in a motel somewhere along the way. The total trip was 5000 km, and we were towing our little motor boat, an aluminium dinghy. Tegshee had picked out a cheap rental property in Shelley, and the idea was that William would go back to his old primary school and in due course on to the Rossmoyne senior high school when he turned twelve. I would return to Mt Isa by myself and carry on there until I could find a job back in Perth.

We collected the keys for our new residence, and I uncoupled the boat and we were pushing it in to our new back garden. Suddenly I gave a yelp and collapsed on the ground, my left leg all twisted up underneath me. I realised that I had broken my femur, grabbed

2 The City of Joy, by Dominic Lapierre, Arrow Books, 1986

my mobile phone and rang for an ambulance. A neighbour from next door, Roger, came running in to help, and held my head off the bricks until the ambulance arrived. They took me off to a fairly new hospital nearby, the Fiona Stanley hospital. My leg was put in tension, and after a few days on my back they said they would bolt me up in a couple of days. I had had a very unusual fracture, a clean diagonal split from just above the knee to within about six inches of my hip. "By the way" I said. "Before I left Mt Isa, I had a funny bruise above my knee - did you see anything on the X-rays? They told me they would check and shortly after I was given a CAT scan, an MRI, and a biopsy. They came to give me the bad news, which was that I had a lymphoma in the marrow of my femur, which had weakened the bone and caused it to split! How lucky I was that this had not happened while driving over the Nullarbor Plain in South Australia, a 687 mile stretch of essentially straight road running east-west in the middle of nowhere! I would have had to lie there for hours until a Flying Doctor plane could come to rescue me.

Now that the cancerous tumour had been discovered, I had to transfer to another hospital, the Sir Charles Gairdner, where they had a specialist orthopaedic oncology group. Their lead surgeon Professor Richard Carey-Smith was away on annual holidays, so I spent another two weeks on my back. Tegshee was wonderful and came every day to see me with William, and I had my operation.

All but the last three inches of my femur was removed, and I was fitted with a stainless steel rod that was glued into the end of my femur close to the hip. The other end went down to an artificial knee, that was tapped down into the tibia of my left leg. The day following the operation, the surgical team came to see me, and told me it had all been very successful. I smiled and said "Great! When can I go back to work?" They moved a bit closer, and one of them said "In six months?"

I nearly screamed back at them "What? You can't be serious!" But of course they were right. I had to learn to walk again, and had two weeks in a rehabilitation hospital firstly using a walking frame, and then graduating to crutches before I was allowed to go home where I then had to learn to walk without crutches. I also had to have six cycles of chemotherapy. This made my food taste either tasteless or strange, made me sleepless, and all my hair fell out, including eyelashes and all the short and curlies. Again, Tegshee who is a trained Mongolian nurse with ten years of experience looked after me wonderfully well and nursed me back to health. So by the time I was cleared to go back to Mt Isa, it was late November. Glencore were very good to me and gave me three months of extended sick leave. In the meantime I had realised that I could not manage our house in Mt Isa by myself and also put in a 10-hour shift five days a week, so I had found another job which I did not have to start until the end of January. I finished off in Mt Isa and got our house ready for occupation by tenants. William and Tegshee came out to Mt Isa and helped me finish off over Christmas.

While I was recovering from this episode, of course I did a lot of thinking about why this had happened to me. The answer I came up with was from the teachings of Sai Baba. It had happened because of my karma. In a previous life I had probably caused or contributed to a serious leg injury on an old man, and now I had to experience a similar type of suffering. Karma is normally unavoidable and inexorable, and can only be alleviated by divine grace. The Buddhist religion focusses closely on the suffering which we humans experience, and the reasons for it. The good thing about suffering is that the more of it we can suck up, the less we carry forward with us into the next incarnation. We are far more likely to learn while we are suffering than when we are having a good time!

The job in Malaysia was a two-year contract, and my gold mine laboratory team of local Malaysians was a good bunch of people and I taught them everything I could. But the FIFO roster was not at all friendly, six weeks on and only two weeks off, and very hard on my wife Tegshee and son William back in Perth. I resigned at the end of January 2019 to take up better-paid contracts in Perth.

It's now 2021 and we have survived the COVID 19 virus pandemic so far.

# 15

# MY INTEREST IN THE OCCULT

When I was a small boy growing up in Shanklin, Isle of Wight, my mother would sometimes do tea leaf readings for friends. The person would drink their tea, leaving the tea leaves at the bottom of the cup. My mother would then examine the pattern of the tea leaves and make pronouncements about future events for that person, like "You will be going on a journey over the water….", even when we all knew that this was most likely to be a half-hour trip on the ferry that ran between Portsmouth and the Isle of Wight in southern England. All good harmless fun!

My grandfather James Keeley was a Methodist parson, and was in fact the minister in charge of the Shanklin Methodist church until he retired. So I was christened there. Later on when I was teenager I also found out that my grandparents and their friends were also spiritualists, and believed in the existence of unseen spirit entities. They would hold seances, and at times made unwanted contact with evil spirits who scared the hell out of them. My grandparents' interest in spirits was only known within the family and by a few of their very close friends, as the Christian churches for some reason or other regarded any communication with any kind of spirit as essentially bad. This is all a bit odd, as several Christian churches have procedures for conducting exorcism rites, so they certainly believe in the existence of spirits.

This lesson about not contacting spirits was forcibly brought home to an Anglican priest, who was the curator of the ruins of the early Christian abbey at Glastonbury in Somerset as described in the British serial magazine, 'The Occult'. At the time there were only relics of the original construction, most of the abbey having disappeared many years earlier. The priest realised that there must have been many other buildings, accommodation for the monks and nuns, stables for horses etc. So he arranged for a session with a trance channeler to ask questions about the abbey complex hoping to get answers from the spirit of one of the monks who had been based there. The channeler went into a trance and scribbled furiously on a pad as the answers came through to him. One of the questions concerned the identity of a probable noble person whose grave had been found in the grounds of the abbey. This individual was very tall, and he had a wound to his collar bone on one side that had healed up. Between his feet they had found the skull of another man.

After the séance the channeler's writing was examined. It was found to be in an ancient written form of Latin, as the channeler had got through to the spirit of a monk who had lived at Glastonbury. The position of many of the disappeared buildings was given, and the information was checked and confirmed to be correct by trenching, allowing the foundations of the other old buildings to be excavated.

The tall man's name was given, and he was the Lord of the Manor in that area. He had been challenged to a duel by another man, whom he successfully killed, and the skull belonged to the challenger. A check was made with the Domesday Book, dating from the 11$^{th}$ century after the Norman conquest, which gave the Lord of the Manor's name at that time. Again, the information written by the trance chaneller was correct.

Then the curator made a great mistake. He wrote an article about how he had made the miraculous discovery of the former buildings. The Anglican church was not amused. Firstly he was relieved of his duties, and then subsequently sacked.

Later in the early 1970s, my then wife Raelene and I were living in Mt Isa, a mining town in north-west Queensland. With a colleague and his wife we were exploring the use of a ouija board.

The 26 letters of the alphabet were written on small squares of paper, which were then arranged in a circle. A small upturned shot glass was placed in the middle of the circle. We then each put a finger on top of the shot glass, and I asked "Is there anybody there?"

The glass began to move by itself, and moved over to point to various letters around the circle. We wrote the letters down, which said "Message for Mike". The spirit then pointed out more letters, spelling out the following message: "You will buy a carry cot before Christmas."

I looked at my wife who seemed amused. It was already November, and my wife was not pregnant.

We asked the entity what his name was, and the answer was Graham. We then asked Graham what had happened to him, and he told us that his neck had been stretched! At this point we decided that we didn't really want to dabble any more, and said goodbye to Graham.

It was early in the following year, around February, and I suddenly said to my wife "Good Lord! We *did* buy a carry cot before Christmas!" The wife of a colleague at work had a baby just before Christmas, and we decided to buy something useful for them as a gift, not just something cuddly like a teddy bear. So we bought a carry cot for the new baby, and Graham's prediction came true.

In 1976 myself, Raelene and young son Alexander were living in Capel where I worked as the Research Metallurgist at a heavy mineral sands concentrator. In August we put our furniture into store, and went over to London as I had been promised a scholarship to do a PhD degree in Mineral Technology by Prof. Cohen at Imperial College. My mother had agreed that we could stay at her house in

Guibal Road in Lee, south-east London while doing this research study.

About early 1979, I was beginning to doubt whether I would successfully complete my PhD degree, and was wondering whether I should give up and go and get a proper job, so that we would no longer have to survive on my student grant. I had been reading with interest a book about an ancient Chinese divinatory technique called the I Ching[3,4]. The original Chinese procedure was very complicated and involved throwing a bunch of fine yarrow plant sticks up in the air, and then picking them up one at a time in a certain way to create a hexagram, a symbol made of two trigrams, each of three horizontal lines. The lines could either be Yang, unbroken, or Yin, and split into two halves. The modern western way to consult the I Ching is to get three small coins, say 5c or 10c pieces, clasp them in two hands and shake them around, then open your hands and let them drop onto the table in front of you. Depending on how the coins land (e.g. two heads and one tail; two tails and one head, three tails, or three heads) the reference book told me whether I had thrown a yin line or a yang line.

While throwing the coins for the six lines of my hexagram I was thinking intently about my problem, which I framed as a question - “Will I successfully be able to complete my PhD?” I threw my hexagram, and then went to the reference book to interpret my answer. There are 64 possible hexagrams that can be thrown while using the I Ching. I looked up the hexagram that I had thrown, and was blown away by the first line of the commentary, which said “Success Is inevitable!”. So I continued my PhD study, and was awarded my PhD in January 1980.

Trying to think rationally about the I Ching, and what possible connection there might be between the landing face of some tossed coins, and a particular individual’s situation and problems at a specific

3 I Ching (The Richard Wilhelm Translation)with foreword by C.G Jung

4 The Everyday I Ching, by Sarah Dening

point in time, it is very tempting to confidently reply that there is NO possible connection! However the ancient Chinese philosophy of the Tao, considers that the whole of existence (including us) is part of a flowing 'river', that just like a real river has eddies and whirlpools and cataracts along its journey to the ocean. We are all part of this stream, and everything is connected to everything else in this way.

It was while studying for my Ph.D. degree that a fellow post-grad introduced me to the meditation technique known as Transcendental Meditation, [TM]. Barry was doing a Ph.D. in geology and somehow in our friendly chats he found out that I was interested in levitation, and he told me that he could do it! So of course I wanted to know how. So he told me that it was a special course that you could do, but a pre-requisite was to learn the Transcendental Meditation technique taught by TM instructors. The teaching itself came from Maharishi Mahesh Yogi, an Indian spiritual teacher at that time living in Switzerland, where he had established a university. So I signed up, and for a moderate fee I was given the basic TM training by a lovely young woman who was a TM instructor. I found the TM technique very restful, and an excellent way to relax when stressed or tired. During the induction I was given a mantra, a single word which is repeated again and again sub-vocally while meditating for 20 minutes. Ideally this is done twice a day, once in the morning and again in the early evening.

Barry had done an advanced TM course and told me that when using a specific mantra he would rise off the ground, but could not stay levitated yet. So he and other trainees did it on a mattress so they did not hurt themselves when they came down again. I never saw him doing it, and indeed they did not do it in public. But I do have a photograph of a senior lecturer in mathematics from a major university in NSW, who had his photo printed in The Australian newspaper while levitating. Sitting cross-legged, his shoelaces and trouser cuffs hung down below the rest of his body, and so I was satisfied that the photo was genuine, and that he was not just sitting on an invisible glass plate. I was impressed by the fact that this senior academic at a major university had chosen to expose himself to the public ridicule of his university colleagues. Levitation seems to defy the presently known laws of physics, but is a long-time and well-known attribute of Buddhist monks and Indian gurus. Eventually our physics will catch up I am sure to explain this phenomenon.

My own father told me that while in the British Army in India he witnessed the Indian Rope Trick. In this the magician throws up a rope from the ground, standing up straight like a timber pole, and his boy assistant then climbs up it and sits at the top. The boy then climbs down the rope and the magician clicks his fingers and the rope collapses back to the ground. The popular debunk of this magic demonstration is that the people in the audience are hypnotised by the magician, and believe that they have seen the boy climb up the rope and back down again.

But how do you explain the exploits of the British magician Dynamo, whose filmed exploits include floating up in the air, walking on the river Thames, and putting a mobile phone inside an empty Coke bottle, where it can then be heard to ring? You can hypnotise an audience, but you can't hypnotise a video camera.

Some of Dynamo's films shown on Australian television were shot in India, and include changing the length of cotton rags into a long silk sari with a single flick; making a pile of papers spontaneously ignite; and making a few candle lights floating on the River Ganges at night suddenly multiply to cover the full width of the river.

Dynamo seems to have mastered the Siddhis, the magical skills developed by the gurus of India. Some of them are described in the book by Paramhansa Yogananda in his 'Autobiography of a Yogi'. [5] There are about eight siddhis, including making yourself invisible, taking a deadly poison but neutralising it and surviving, walking through walls, levitating, being seen and witnessed simultaneously in two different cities, curing a major injury like instantly healing

---

5 Autobiography of a Yogi, by Paramhansa Yogananda

a severed arm, walking on water, and manifesting things like coins out of thin air.

Wolf Messing, the Jewish psychic who was the personal assistant and clairvoyant to Stalin, had met Sai Baba during his travels in India. Later he was challenged by Stalin to get past the security guards at three successive security gates to gain entry to Stalin's private dacha. This he successfully did, possibly by using the siddhi for invisibility, so that he could walk straight pass the guards.

The British authors of the book entitled "The Holy Blood and the Holy Grail" [6]believe that Jesus, in the unrecorded gap between his exploits as a boy in the temple at Jerusalem and taking up his ministry as a man, travelled to India where he studied with the yogis and learnt how to materialise the loaves and fishes; walk on water to save his fishermen disciples in the storm; heal the sick, blind and cripples; and heal the spear wound in his side which he suffered during his crucifixion. Further they state that after the crucifixion, he returned to what is now Kashmir. His tomb in Srinigar is known as the tomb of Saint Issa, and the mould of his feet shows the holes of the nails that fixed his feet to the cross.

In 1981 I was working at BHP's Central Research Laboratory in Newcastle, NSW. Most of the work done at this laboratory related to the processing of low-grade coals, although research on some other commodities like manganese ores was also conducted. A vacancy developed in Whyalla, South Australia, where they needed a metallurgist who was very familiar with base metals. I applied for a transfer and was given it, and became the Metallurgist in Charge of the Whyalla Laboratory. No coal work was done here, but rather the work was mainly focussed on iron ores and special tests for the blast furnace and the iron ore pellet plant, plus some work on copper-gold, gold and tin ores.

---

[6] The Holy Blood and the Holy Grail, by Richard Lee, Michael Baigent and Henry Lincoln

While in Whyalla I took up the opportunity to join the Rosicrucians, a mystical group that has teachings about for example clairvoyance, telepathy, intuition, and the health effects on the body of certain musical sounds. This teaching was done by posted lessons, and it wasn't until after I moved back to Perth in late 1982 that I was able to physically join one of their groups. Famous Rosicrucians include the British scientist Sir Isaac Newton, and also the amazing musical composer, Mozart. I am not a great fan of opera, but of the operas that I love, Mozart's 'The Magic Flute' is my favourite. Other Rosicrucians of Mozart's day strongly criticised Mozart as they believed that in The Magic Flute, Mozart revealed too much of the Rosicrucians' secret knowledge.

In 1987 I went to see a clairvoyant in Fremantle near Perth, Western Australia. The man's name was John, and he was very thorough. First he inked the palms of both hands on a big black inking pad, and then each hand was pressed onto a piece of white A4 paper from which he read the lines on my palms. I did not take any notes but the general gist was that I would have a very long and mainly healthy life. Intriguingly, he also advised me that I was 'on a quest!'

He then brought out a Tarot pack, which has four suits of 14 cards each as in a normal game of cards, the so-called Minor Arcana. The four suits in the Minor Arcana are not the familiar Hearts, Clubs, Diamonds and Spades. Instead they are Swords, Rods, Pentacles and Cups. In addition there are a further 22 cards with archetypal pictures on them, the Major Arcana. The pictures include the Emperor, The Empress, the High Priestess, the Lovers, Death, the Fool and so on.

As part of the reading, I personally shuffled and cut the whole pack, and then chose ten cards face down that were then laid out face up in a special order by the clairvoyant.

I have forgotten the details of most of the reading, except for one part that subsequently totally blew me away. John picked up a card, of a dark queen, and told me he thought that this represented my mother. "How is your mother?' he asked. I told him that my mother was over in London, England, but that we wrote to each other every few months, and as far as I knew she was well. He then said that he was very sorry to tell me this, but he thought that my mother was very seriously ill. He then went on with the rest of his reading.

After this session, I didn't give his warning a great deal of thought. However, almost exactly a week later I received a telegram from my Uncle Russell, a medical doctor in UK. The telegram told me that my mother had had an unsuccessful operation and was now dying of cancer. If I wanted to see her alive before she died I would have to fly to England immediately.

I had just signed a new employment contract with an old friend Ron Butler who was Managing Director of a mineral consultancy in Sydney, New South Wales. I explained the situation to him and cancelled the contract, then booked a flight to London and was met at London airport by Russell, who took me to his home. We went to the hospice where my mother was in palliative care. She looked very gaunt, but was able to speak, and she thanked me for coming. On the next couple of visits she was asleep, and seemed to know that we were praying for her. "Let me go" she whispered. The next day we got a call from the hospice. My mother was no longer with us. We went and saw her lying naked and contorted on the bed, waiting to be taken to the funeral parlour. My uncle closed her eyes, and a funeral parlour man came in a suit, and removed her platinum wedding ring, which was never recovered.

We went home to Russell's house and he read me her will with my Aunt Barbara present. Uncle Russell was the executor of my mother's will. My two sons, Alex and Lincoln, were each to get GBP 20,000 when her house was sold, but would not be able to get a penny of it until they were thirty years old, and their funds would be placed in a trust run by Russell's daughter Janet, a lawyer. The rest of the proceeds were to be divided up among about fourteen relatives, and I was to get GBP 2000 which didn't even cover half of my airfare.

I told my Aunt and Uncle that the purpose of life was not to inherit wealth from one's relatives - it had to be something far, far grander than that. I also said that since I was now unemployed, my first duty was to get back to my wife and sons in Perth, and find a job. So I did not stay a further week until her cremation service, but caught the first plane back to Perth that I could find, sending a mass of red roses as a wreath for her funeral.

I decided not to contest the will, even though I was the only child, and I certainly didn't relish the prospect of wasting money to fight my own relatives in court. Overall both my father and my mother had been wonderful parents, who made sacrifices to give me the best possible education.

In 1990 my marriage broke down, and my wife Raelene and I went for counselling. It was clear that there was no way we could keep living harmoniously together, so I left and moved into a temporary flat. Raelene rejected my maintenance offer, and instead applied for Child Support which in those days meant that 21% of my gross salary was deducted at source before tax. The divorce was finalised two years later, the standard waiting time. Our family home was to be sold, and she would get 80%, myself 20%. And so it was, and I continued to maintain my sons until they were 18, and even longer for the younger boy Lincoln who had to do an extra year at high school in order to matriculate.

After my marriage breakdown I was rather lost and confused, and arranged to visit a clairvoyant. I arrived at the appointment and found that there were two clairvoyants there, an old lady who was a trance channeler and a younger woman. The old lady went into a trance, and gave me a reading in a different voice. I don't remember the exact advice, only that it made sense at the time. Then the younger lady examined my palms, and finished up with a tarot reading. In summing up, they recommended me to attend a spiritualist church, and gave me the contact details for the Minister who ran the group. Together they both advised me that I would have a guru. "That's nice' I said politely, and asked how I would recognise my guru if I saw him in the street. "Oh, you'll have no trouble recognising him at all" they said. So I asked what he looked like, and was told that he was a little Indian man and that he wore an orange tunic. My first reaction was to reject this, although I said nothing at the time. In Perth at that time there was a group who called themselves the Orange Order, and they wore orange clothes. Their guru was the Indian, Baghwan Shri Rajneesh, whose headquarters were at Poona in India. He was reputed to encourage free sex among his devotees, but I have no idea whether this was true or not.

Anyway, I took up the suggestion to visit the spiritualist church, which was in a suburb called Southern River. The normal Christian hymns were sung at the services, the music being played on a quivery piano. The pastor was an accomplished painter, and his paintings were displayed in the entrance hall. In the church itself in a central position was a huge and amazing painting of Armageddon. It depicted two adjoining countries somewhere in the Middle East, separated by a gulf of water with patrolling submarines, and with each side pointing missiles at the other. High above in the sky, in the middle of a circle of winged angels stood Jesus, watching the stand-off below.

I got to know the people in the spiritualist group, and we used to have distant healing sessions for people not able to be present, and also sessions for sick people who attended. We would direct our palms towards them and send healing prayers and hopefully healing energy towards them.

At one of the healing sessions, a lady told me that she had just come back from India, and had a wonderful video about a guru there called Sai Baba, and asked me if I would like to go to her place and see it. I had already seen videos of the faith healers in the Philippines, who plunge their bare hands into the patient's body, pull bits of diseased tissue out and then invisibly seal the incision by running their finger along it. Anyway, I decided not to go, but thanked her.

The church also used to have regular flower readings. The idea was that if you needed some guidance, you went to your garden and cut a beautiful flower like a rose, while thinking intently about your problem, or the thing you wanted an answer to.

You then went to the church hall and laid your flower on a special table, along with other flowers laid by other people. With everyone attending, the clairvoyant would then arrive, and after greeting the attendees would then at random select a flower from the table, feeling the vibrations of the person who had laid it there. She would then give her advice, the person sitting in the audience knowing that the message for this flower was for them. The clairvoyant would then select another flower, and give her next reading. I attended several times to get my own flower readings, and although the advice was general it was specific enough to be relevant for the problem I wanted guidance on.

On one particular evening a different kind of clairvoyant medium came, to give messages to people who wanted to talk to the spirits of their relatives who had passed on. The lights were dimmed and I was sitting close to the back. Despite the near darkness, the medium's eyes had a silvery glow, and I nudged the person next to me and in a whisper, asked why the medium's eyes were shining. "They are the eyes of spirit" I was told.

When my divorce from Raelene came through in 1992, I met and later married a Polish woman named Alicia. Some time later in early 1994 I resigned from my job for Western Mining in Perth, and we moved to Sydney where I had landed a very good job with a company called Savage Resources, owners of the copper-gold deposit at Ernest Henry, about 130 km north of the town of Cloncurry in north-west Queensland. It was in Sydney that the prediction made by the two lady clairvoyants about acquiring a guru really started to take shape.

But the marriage to Alicia slowly deteriorated, and I found that she had thrown away many of my technical journals from a packing box that was originally full and heavy, despite her denials. It seemed that she was jealous of any interest I took in anything that was other to herself. Later I found that she was using part of my salary to pay off the residential unit that she still owned in her own name back in Perth. Eventually I realised that I was just her milking cow, and had also gotten sick of all our unnecessary endless rows. So I left her.

In Perth I had a friend who was a Sai Baba devotee. Anna had been unwell for a time, had no energy, and her doctor could not find anything wrong with her. Anna had a friend living in Solo on the island of Java who was a Javanese princess, and Anna went to Solo for a holiday with her. Together they went to meditate at a syncretist temple. While they were sitting meditating, Anna noticed that some of the other meditators were scowling at her. She whispered a question to her Javanese friend who asked her to wait until the meditation was complete. When the session was finished, Anna and her friend conferred with the priest. He explained that the other meditators had seen a black serpent coiled around her neck, with its head pointing down as if to strike her on the head. The priest asked Anna if she had been dabbling in black magic. "Absolutely not" said Anna, "I never have anything to do with that kind of stuff". The priest asked "Are you sure? Think very carefully!" Anna thought very carefully, and remembered when she had been invited to a party in Claremont, a fairly swanky Perth suburb. Arriving at the house and going into the entrance hall, she noticed that the walls were painted black. Black cat figurines were placed on shelves. She was shown into the party room where naked people were dancing around a fire in the centre of the room. Realising that some kind of black magic ceremony was going on, Anna immediately turned to leave. "I'm sorry but this is not my scene", she said. The hostess was very concerned and said "Oh, but please, you must stay! We want you to stay!" Anna refused and as she left she could see that the hostess was very angry.

The priest explained that the hostess had put a curse on Anna, which was the cause of her sickness, and said he would get a priestess to conduct a cleansing rite. The priestess commenced the cleansing rite, but before it was complete she ran off screaming. The priest then reappeared and explained that the priestess had been chased away by demons. He then completed a cleansing rite himself. Anna then immediately felt better, and her health was restored.

Another friend I met in Perth who was an Italian told me about a different kind of brush he had had with black magic in Perth. Luigi was having some renovations done to his house in Fremantle, and before the job was complete, the Sicilian contractors demanded full payment. My friend said he would be happy to pay them once the job was completed. Then Luigi and his wife had endless sleepless nights because every time they went to bed, it sounded like a dog was chasing a cat around above the ceiling in their bedroom. Luigi went up in the roof cavity to see what was there but found nothing, and the scampering noises continued relentlessly. Finally Luigi got a long extension ladder and put it up outside against the high roof of the house. To his amazement he saw that in each corner of the gutter around the roof, someone had put an egg! Luigi put on rubber gloves, and collected the four eggs in a plastic bucket, then took them down to the beach and threw them into the sea. Instantly the scampering noises stopped, and they were able to sleep normally again.

# 16

# GAINING A GURU

In Sydney after my break-up with Alicia, I started to make new friends, one of whom told me that there was a marvellous clairvoyant whose name was Alan Pilkington, who lived at that time in Brisbane in Queensland, but who used to come down to Sydney now and again to give readings to clients. He was famous for making long term predictions that were accurate and sometimes took as long as four years to be fulfilled.

I managed to get Alan's phone number, and rang him to make an appointment at the hotel where he had taken a room for his consultations. He was a little friendly man, and came down in the lift to meet me. As we travelled up in the lift to go to his room, he blew me away by saying "You've just had a very serious marriage break-up!"

Once we were in his room, he gave me more details. "Your ex used to attack you psychically, and she will use every trick in the book to get you back! But whatever you do, you must resist! Do not go back to her!"

With this serious stuff out of the way, we talked about other things. I noticed a broad gold ring on his finger, set with a large and rather murky-coloured green stone. Because of my interest in gem stones, I asked him what the stone was, and he told me that it was a diamond. A green diamond! I asked to have a look at it, and he held out his hand. The stone was certainly cut like a diamond, and I asked him where he got this amazing ring from. "My guru manifested it for me" said Alan, so I said "Who is your guru?" Alan told me that his guru was Baghwan Sri Sathya Sai Baba in India, and I did not have to ask who Sai Baba was, because I had previously read Howard Murphet's book called "Man of Miracles"[7] while I was still living back in Perth. The cover shows Sai Baba, wearing his characteristic Afro hair style, and wearing an orange tunic!

I told Alan that I knew about Sai Baba and would be interested to join a Sai group in Sydney if there was one. Alan said he would check and let me know. Sure enough, a few days later I had a visit to my Sydney office from a man who gave me contact details for the local group in Hurstville, a suburb in the south-west of Sydney where I was living. He also gave me a little packet of vibhuti, a grey, holy ash, made at Sai Baba's ashram at Puttaparthi in India. A few days later I rang the contact given me in Hurstville and joined the Sai group there. The members were mainly Indians, with a light sprinkling of Westerners. The group members made me very welcome. We would sing bhajans, a bit like the hymns in a Christian church, except that in many of the bhajans the words were all in Sanskrit and the chants were full of the names of the Indian deities like Shiva and Ganesha, the elephant-headed deity. There were bhajans in English too, and the singing was accompanied by dexterous harmonium playing augmented at times by vigorous tabla drumming.

One of the practices was to chant the 108 different names of God, in Sanskrit. I always wondered why there were 108, instead of say 109 or 110! It was only many years later that I received a satisfactory explanation, from a Hindu who was the Chief Accountant at a gold mine I worked at in Malaysia. The explanation reminded me strongly of the western belief in sacred geometry and gematria (number magic) to explain the diameter of the orbits of

---

7 Sai Baba - Man of Miracles by Howard Murphet, World of Books

the planets in the solar system. The explanation was this: if you take the distance between the surface of the earth and the surface of the moon, the diameter of the moon goes into that distance 108 times. Similarly if you take the distance between the surface of the sun and the surface of the earth, the earth's diameter goes into that distance 108 times. Of course, the moon's orbit around the earth is not perfectly spherical, and similarly the earth's orbit around the sun is not completely spherical. But I checked the figures and found that they were indeed approximately correct.

On one occasion we were chanting the 108 names of God using the light from hundreds of tiny little candles. A few trays of unlit candles were sitting on a table. During the chanting, one of the unlit candles spontaneously lit itself, sending a gasp from the devotees who saw it happen.

My stay in Sydney came to an end unexpectedly, as I was told by my employer that I was to be retrenched in six week's time. Fortunately I was able to use this time to look around for another Sydney-based job, but there was nothing available. So I wrote to Sai Baba at his ashram in India and asked him to help me quickly find another job. On a hunch, I rang Rio Tinto's offices in Melbourne, and was directed to ring their Advanced Technical Development Laboratory at Bundoora.

The manager was away when I rang, so I left a message for him, without really expecting him to reply. To my amazement a few days later he rang me and asked me to send him my CV, which I sent by email. A couple of days later he asked if I could go down for an interview, which he was willing to give me on a Saturday morning! So I flew down to Melbourne on a Friday evening, had my interview on the Saturday morning, and was offered a job on the spot. On the Monday I was back at work in Sydney without my colleagues even realising that I had been away. I could then arrange for all my furniture to be collected by a removalist, and cancelled my flat lease. On the last day at work in Sydney I said goodbye to my Sydney colleagues and caught a plane down to Melbourne and moved to a motel where Rio Tinto had booked me a week's accommodation while I looked for a new flat. So I had lost my job, found a new one in a different state, and didn't even suffer a single day of unpaid work.

On another occasion I attended a group meditation while a bell was rung by rubbing a rod against the inside rim until the sound got louder and louder before it suddenly stopped. There was then a rustling sound like someone rubbing silk cloth together, and fresh, chopped rose petals materialised above our heads and fell down on top of us. I collected some of the petal fragments and took them home, and after a few days they turned brown.

Down in Melbourne in 1996 I found a new flat in Rosanna, which was quite close to Rio Tinto's laboratory. I then looked round for a local Sai group and found one fairly quickly. The leader at that time was a Sinhalese man called Dayal, and about 6 months later he organised a visit to Sai Baba's ashram in Andhra Pradesh. I realised that now was my opportunity to see Sai Baba myself, so I registered for the group tour. There were about 30 of us and we flew from Melbourne to Chennai and spent the night at a hotel. The next day we flew to Bangalore in the middle of India to the west where we again spent the night in a hotel. From Bangalore we took a group of taxi vans the further 400km to Puttaparthi where we stayed in the ashram accommodation. As a group we all wore white cotton uniforms, together with our Melbourne group badge. We had several families with us in our group. One couple got a family room as they had their small baby with them. The mother took a shower one afternoon, and put on a new uniform. She then realised that her badge was still fixed to the blouse of the uniform she had taken off. When she unpinned it she was amazed to find that a photograph of Sai Baba had materialised on the back of her badge, as shown in the picture below.

Picture of Sai Baba materialised on the back of the badge

We attended the daily morning sessions at the ashram, which involved getting up very early at around 2.30 a.m., and waiting in line. The leader of each line drew a number concealed in a bag. The line that picked number 1 were the first to go into the hall and get seating right at the front, and our group was lucky enough to be close to the front on several occasions. So I was able to place two letters directly into Sai Baba's hands asking him to bless my two sons, Alex and Lincoln. Sai Baba never had to open the letters - if he accepted the letter it meant that he had accepted the request inside. Sometimes he refused to accept an offered letter, meaning that the contained request was unacceptable to him.

The hall was very large and the devotees were segregated - all the males together and all the females together. The most wonderful thing for me was that I could see Sai Baba's halo, like a ball of flowing soft luminescent light around his head, staying with him as he moved about. He would also manifest sweets and throw them to people to eat, and one day I saw him making a gold ring for one of the student boys who attended the college at the ashram. Sai Baba slipped it on to the boy's finger, and the boy then broke down and sobbed with emotion.

The most amazing experience while I was there concerned a family from Melbourne who arrived about a week after we did. Their daughter had some kind of illness which was treated at the Children's Hospital in Melbourne. The treatment was incorrect and the girl went into a coma, and was kept alive on a drip for six months until the hospital needed her bed for other patients. The parents were supplied with the drip medication and took their daughter home. They had heard about the miraculous cures given by Sai Baba, and decided to take the chance and flew to Chennai. But from Chennai they could not fly to Bangalore, because the internal Indian airline refused to take a passenger in a coma. So by combination of bus and taxi they came to Bangalore, and then again up to Puttaparthi. By the time they arrived, all the money they had brought was gone, so our Sai group members had a whip-round collection to give them enough money to pay for their accommodation. Sai Baba told them that their daughter would be OK and that they should take the drip out and come to the assembly the next morning. I had already made plans to leave the Ashram that very next day, to travel to Kolar in Karnataka state to stay with some very good Indian friends of mine, so I did not see the miracle but was told about it when our group all met up again in Melbourne. Sai Baba went up to the girl and tapped her lightly on the head, and she came out of her coma!

While at Puttaparthi, we visited the new Super Specialty Hospital set up by Sai Baba to give free medical aid to the poor people in the surrounding state. From the outside it looks like a Maharaja's palace, built of soft-pink stone and with a dome and narrow towers. Inside it is all marble flooring and air conditioning. Overseas surgeons and specialists visit the hospital from all over the world to donate their services.

The Super-Specialty Hospital at Puttaparthi

The story of the hospital is amazing. Isaac Tigrett, co-founder of the Hot Rock café franchise, donated the required funds to Sai Baba. An American hospital construction company was called in for a meeting with Sai Baba, who said that he wanted the hospital to be up, running and performing its first operation in exactly one year from the day of the meeting. The consultants laughed, and said that it would take at least a year just to draw the plans! But exactly one year later, the hospital performed its first operation.

Some years later after my trip to Putthaparti, around 2002, I was working in Auckland, New Zealand, where I was teaching English to Asian students, mainly Chinese and Koreans and occasionally Japanese.

One of my fellow teachers was an Indian lady who had obtained her teaching degree at the Sathya Sai University at Puttaparthi. In conversing, she discovered that I was a Sai devotee, and invited me to her house for afternoon tea one weekend. Her wedding had been hosted by Sai Baba, who also fed all the guests. More than that, he materialised her engagement ring and her wedding ring. She showed me the photos taken at her wedding, and I could see that the rings in the wedding photos were exactly the same as the rings she was still wearing. Was she lying to me? I think absolutely not.

At three separate houses of Sai devotees, I have witnessed another of Sai Baba's leelas, a kind of little miracle that science cannot explain. Two of these houses were in Melbourne, Victoria, and the third in Perth, Western Australia.

The devotees in question all had a little shrine to Sai Baba in their house, with pictures of Sai Baba, his predecessor Shirdi Sai Baba, Shiva, Jesus and other gods from the Hindu spiritual tradition. The pictures were small, wooden-framed pictures covered by glass. On the glass there is a grey powdery growth of vibhuti, the holy ash, scattered in irregular clumps. It has a beautiful and unique perfume, reminiscent both of roses and of frangipani flowers. This powder is regularly scraped off and given in little paper packets to shrine visitors, only to grow slowly back again!

If I had not personally seen these things, I would regard them as nonsense of course.

In his writings, Sai Baba says that the Earth is unique in the universe. To be born in a human body is the result of merit gained in many, many lifetimes. Even angels and archangels would love to have the opportunity to be born on earth in a human body! The reason is this: Only a human soul can evolve spiritually to the point where they can merge directly with God. If you are now just an angel, you are stuck in that position for eternity!

My acceptance of Sai Baba's teachings and of religions other than the one I was brought up in has helped me to understand more about Christianity, including some of Christ's sayings.

"Should someone smite you on the cheek, turn the other cheek": This seems crazy, and goes against the temptation to hit the offending person back so hard that he will never bother you again! But unfortunately there is a karmic price to pay for such retaliation, the inevitable reaction to your action. The only way to avoid this addition to your karmic debt is to avoid retaliation, and at most just block and neutralise the incoming strike. Think of the famous

Sicilian vendettas, where a cycle of killings and pay-back killings goes on forever. The only way to stop this? Turn the other cheek!

"Blessed are the meek, for they shall inherit the earth!": We don't know what Christ actually said, and it is well known that many translating errors were made from the Aramaic of the original writings. But what Christ may have meant is that your spiritual descendants in their follow-on incarnations would inherit the earth.

"Render unto Caesar that which is Caesar's": Stop complaining about your taxes, because whoever is in power, you will need to pay your taxes!

"Those who live by the sword will die by the sword": Collecting your karma in this lifetime! Possible example, the American Sniper, Chris Kyle.

While what happened to Chris Kyle is considered to be a tragedy for this American hero and his family, we can still celebrate his heroism. We all have to die! But our spirit does not die, and will live again in our next incarnation.

17

# COINCIDENCES?

It was some time in the late 80s, and I was driving into the city of Perth for a meeting, in fact it was for a job interview. Like many modern cities, Perth has one of those annoying and frustrating one-way traffic systems, although fortunately not every street is affected.

To get to the car park for which I was aiming, I headed up the main street which ran north-west from the Causeway Bridge. Close to the river, it's called Adelaide Terrace, then half-way up, it becomes St Georges Terrace which climbs towards an imposing false archway behind which the parliament buildings can be seen: the road then abruptly swings off to the left to climb a hill up towards Kings Park. Slightly before climbing the said hill, I took a right turn into Milligan Street, and then another right turn into one-way Murray Street. This would bring me down to the rear entrance of His Majesty's car park, a spiral ramp affair which you entered at street level before going upwards in seemingly endless circles until a vacant parking spot materialised. As I passed down Murray Street, I glanced at a new car park which had recently opened, and drove past. The entry sign of the car park I wanted loomed: "CAR PARK FULL", it said in big neon letters! Blast! I resignedly continued down to William Street, turned right and then right again into St Georges Terrace, to go around the loop again.

Now running late for my job interview, I pulled off Murray Street into the new car park, which was almost empty, and found a vacant spot almost immediately.

Locking the car, I made for what I hoped was the exit into Murray Street. As I got close to the doorway, I noticed a hand-written sign attached to the door handle. "Handle not working. Use other exit", it said. Disbelievingly, I turned the handle and it opened freely, revealing a narrow corridor with a frosted glass door at the end through which I could see the shadowy shapes of passing pedestrians. Going down to this street door I grasped the handle, and you guessed it, it would not budge! Blast! I said again, and returned to the other door, which by now had swung shut. You can imagine my feelings when I saw that there was no handle on the inside! I was trapped in the corridor!

Should I use my karate skills to kick down the door and get back into the car park? Not a good idea, I thought, especially since they had hung a sign there. I would undoubtedly have to pay the bill for repairs. So what about the frosted glass door at the street end? Also not a good idea! Besides, I might get cut in the process.

I decided my best option was to knock very loudly on the frosted glass door, the moment I saw someone starting to walk past, and shout for help.

I stood by the frosted glass door and someone started to walk past. I knocked loudly and in a loud voice cried out "Please help me! I'm locked in a corridor and can't get out! Please go into the car park and ask the attendant to let me out!"

The person, who I couldn't see properly, was a woman. "Okay, Mike, give me a few minutes" she said. "Okay Mike" I thought. Who the hell can it be? I went back to the other door, and a few minutes later heard the patter of approaching footsteps. The door opened and there was the attendant, together with Marina, the office receptionist from my job as Chief of a government laboratory several years earlier. She had recognised my voice through the frosted glass door, even though she could not see me, and she was the very first person to walk past! My ordeal had lasted five minutes.

It was around 1966, probably late 1966, when I was working as an exploration geologist in the Solomon Islands, that another strange 'co-incidence' occurred, which I remember well. I was with CRA Exploration (CRAE), and we were on their mineral exploration ship, the CRAE Star. We were systematically exploring the islands one by one, and were offshore from the island of Santa Isabel. The International Nickel Company (INCO) were working in the area, and had some nickel leases over very dense ultramafic rocks on Santa Isabel island. We decided to say hello to them, and took the CRAE Star into a little bay where their wharf poked out into the sea.

Tying up, we went ashore, and I admired some beautiful little white terns which were fluttering and hovering over the clear waters of the bay. They must be Fairy Terns, I thought, remembering my schoolboy hobby of ornithology which I continued to enjoy around the world when opportunities presented.

We walked up the hill to the locally built wooden house, with plaited bamboo walls and sacsac leaf layers for the roof, and were met by John Earthrowl, the Canadian geologist in charge. John was a hospitable fellow, and in no time we were sitting around the table enjoying some cold beer. After the professional formalities were out of the way, I asked John about the terns. "Could they be Fairy Terns?", I asked. "Indeed they are, said John, but why are you interested?" I told him about my boyhood hobby at my boarding school at Woolverstone in Suffolk, along the banks of the beautiful River Orwell in south-eastern England. "I used to do birdwatching too at my boarding school at Willemshaven in Germany", said John. "That's interesting" I said, "the friend I used to go birdwatching with at Woolverstone had also been previously at school in Willemshaven!" "What was his name", said John. "David Harris", I replied. There was a stunned silence. "Dave was my birdwatching friend at Willemshaven too", said John.

So there we were, two strangers, sitting having a beer on a tiny island on the western edge of the Pacific, and we had both been to school with the same friend on the other side of the world!

A follow-up to this story happened in about 2015, when I was working in Mt Isa in north-west Queensland. I was looking at the webpage of a uranium exploration company on the Internet.

I always look at the names of the directors, to see if there's anyone I already know.

On this occasion, all the directors' names were unfamiliar, but they had a guy listed as their technical consultant, by the name of John Earthrowl! It must be the same geologist I met on Santa Isabel I thought, and I left a message for him at the company's contact email address. A few days later I received a phone call from John, and I introduced myself, and asked if he had been on Santa Isabel in 1966. "Indeed I was", said John, "but how did you know that?" I then told him about the visit to his camp by the CRAE geologists and he remembered. More amazingly he was still in regular touch with Dave Harris, our mutual friend in London. Today John is retired and lives near Devonport in Tasmania, where he and his wife farm a type of fruit called feijoas.

It is experiences like this that convince me that what we perceive as "coincidences" are God's way of demonstrating to us that he knows absolutely everything about everyone, as indeed you would expect him to!

I have come to the view that co-incidences, when considered as a random, chance event, do not exist, since nothing happens by chance, and everything has a cause.

If you open your front door and a brown, dead leaf is there on your doorstep, it is not there by chance, and it is not there because you planned it. It is there because it grew on a tree somewhere in your local neighbourhood, and after it died and a wind came along that caused the stem to break off, it was caught by the swirling wind. Knowing the direction of the wind gust and with an aerodynamic model of the leaf's shape, with a suitably smart aerodynamic software package on your computer, you could predict that this leaf would land on your doorstep. It is there because it had to be there!

Many years ago I read an amazing true story in a little monthly magazine called the Reader's Digest, which is still published today. It was about a police superintendent in Honolulu, Hawaii, who had the seemingly magical skill of solving unsolvable cases. Relying on my memory, the story went like this.

A traffic cop was driving along the main bay road in Honolulu, following a woman driver. Suddenly she drifted off the road onto a grassy area near the beach and crashed into a bush. The traffic cop also pulled off the road and went over to look at the driver, who was slumped over the wheel.

He opened the car door and noticed that the pupil of her eye was completely expanded. The woman was dead. He examined her quickly while he called for an ambulance. She seemed to be uninjured. The back passenger window of the car, facing out to sea across the bay, was down about one inch from the top.

The ambulance came and took the woman to a major city hospital, where it was confirmed that she was dead. They looked closely for any sign of injury, and finally noticed that she had a clean bullet hole in her head in the crease behind her right ear. An autopsy was conducted and the bullet was extracted.

The homicide case was passed to the police superintendent to solve. He met with his detectives at Police HQ, and together they looked at a big map of Honolulu city. "Where do we start Boss?", asked one of the detectives. The superintendent jabbed with his finger at the corner of a block in the city. "Start here" he instructed.

The detectives arrived at the corner of the city block, which was occupied by a petrol station. They parked and went into the kiosk, where a man was behind the counter.

"Good morning" began one of the detectives, showing his police badge. "We're doing a routine check on firearms. Do you own a firearm?" "Yes" said the man, who was the petrol station owner. "I have a rifle". The detectives asked when the rifle had last been used, and were told the man had been out in the bay fishing for snapper a week before, and had trouble with a shark that was eating his snapper as he tried to pull the line in. The shark was almost at the surface, about 30 feet away. He fired one shot at it and it disappeared. The man pulled his line in and headed back to the shore. "OK", said the detectives, "Just bring your rifle into HQ in the next few days so that we can examine it."

The rifle was presented, and a ballistic firing test was done. The markings on the test bullet were an exact match for the markings on the bullet extracted from the dead woman. The bullet had skipped on the water, gone low across the sea to the coast highway, passed through the open slot in the passing car's back window, and hit the woman behind the ear. More amazingly, the woman was a relative of the man who fired the shot.

Believe it, or not!

# 18

# Reincarnation

Reincarnation is dismissed by many as being a lot of nonsense, but personally I am absolutely convinced that it is part of the reality of our existence, here on planet Earth. It is a fundamental belief of adherents to both Buddhism and the Hindu faith.

Probably the most renowned proof of reincarnation is the 14th Dalai Lama, now living in exile in northern India. It is recorded that as a child of about age three, he was identified by senior Tibetan Lamas who travelled to eastern Tibet to find him, guided by a vision, and asked him to identify pictures of lamas who had died before he was born. They also got him to correctly identify personal items that had belonged to the 13th Dalai Lama at the time of his death, chosen in preference to an almost identical set.

Another renowned example of reincarnation is the US General in charge of the American troops in Europe in the final stages of the Second World War, namely General George S Patton[8]. Earlier, Patton defeated Rommel in North Africa. Patton could read German, and read Rommel's own book on the art of tank warfare. He then set a desert trap for Rommel using the strategies from Rommel's book, and Rommel's troops walked into it, resulting in their capture.

---

8 Patton, by Martin Blumenson, William Morrow Paperbacks,1994

While still in north Africa a subordinate offered to show Patton the battlefield where the Romans inflicted the final military defeat of the Carthaginians in 146 BC, before they also totally destroyed Carthage itself. "It's just over here Sir, a few miles away". "No it's not" said Patton, "It's this way. Come with me and I'll show you!" They got into the jeep and went to the site, and stood on a low hill overlooking the site while Patton gave a blow by blow description of the battle. The subordinate was astounded, and said "but how do you know all this Sir?" Patton replied that it was because he was a Legionnaire in the Roman army, and had fought in that battle.

Many people who believe in reincarnation think that when we die, our spirit does not, as it is of course our spirit that becomes reincarnated. On the spirit plane, we review the lessons that we need to learn, before selecting parents for our next life in the appropriate culture and situation, hopefully to learn the appropriate spiritual lessons in this next life. In this view, the purpose of each life, each incarnation, is to evolve spiritually so that eventually after thousands of repeated lives we can become spiritually advanced enough to be able to merge with God, like raindrops that reach the river and eventually re-unite with the ocean.

Of course, when we reincarnate, generally we remember nothing of our previous lives, and the 14th Dalai Lama who can remember all 13 of his previous incarnations is a rare exception.

But there is a growing literature recorded from people who have 'flashback' remembrances, and an interesting television program shown on Australia's ABC channel in 2020 was about a little boy about five or six years old, living on the Scottish mainland in Glasgow, who spoke sadly to his mother about his previous life on the Scottish island of Barra. He was very insistent, so his mother got psychologists to check him out. They pronounced him as genuine. Eventually to lay the matter to rest, his mother took him to Barra, where he identified the house that he lived in and which fitted all his previous descriptions.

I myself have had a flashback, or at least that is how I interpret it. At the age of 32, I was living in Bunbury, south of Perth in Western Australia. There was a local karate club here, and at last I was able to fulfil my ambition to learn karate, and I joined the Go Ju Karate Club run by Sensei Alan Burdett. From beginner I advanced in Alan's class to 3rd Kyu, the first brown belt. Then I moved back to London, and trained there firstly with another Go Ju Club and then in a Shotokan style Club at the Budokwai, run by Sensei John Anderson, with whom I advanced to 1st Kyu brown belt.

Later I returned to Australia and lived successively in Newcastle NSW, Whyalla SA, Perth WA, Sydney NSW, Melbourne VIC and then again in Perth. Each time I moved, I joined a local karate club, eventually getting my Black Belt in Perth in 1992 at age 50 in the Wado Ryu style. So you can see that although I didn't have any special talent, I kept doing it because I loved it. In fact I only stopped training in 2014 when I was working in Mt Isa, Queensland. The question is WHY!

An answer to this question came to me unexpectedly. I had always admired the Kung Fu skills of the monks at the Shaolin temple in China, and was lucky enough to see them perform at an exhibition in Perth one year.

About 25 years ago I had an incredibly vivid dream in which I was present in the very early morning or perhaps at dusk, standing on the ground and looking up at some strange tall and narrow towers that had little 'mushroom' type roofs placed one above the other at intervals to the top. The air was cold and I could feel its bite on my skin. In this life I have never seen any towers exactly similar, with the exception perhaps of some of the towers at the Hindu temple at Besakhi at the east end of Bali.

Ten years later, I was watching a film on Australian TV on the ABC channel which was about the Shaolin Temple. They showed the monks doing their chanting, their living quarters, and their training ground where both old and young monks displayed their Kung Fu skills. Then they moved to the graveyard at the back of the temple where the dead monks were buried. There on the screen in front of me were the towers that I had seen in my dream! Maybe my bones from a previous life are there at the Shaolin temple!

It is very difficult to believe that a spirit plane exists where only spirit beings reside. Despite the fairy tale quality of this idea, **what if it's actually true**? Trying to imagine it is a bit like imagining the taste of a fruit that you have never seen or eaten. Nevertheless, a belief in such 'other' planes of existence is fundamental to the body of knowledge enshrined in the Jewish Kabbala, where four planes of existence are described: the God plane, the Archangel Plane, the Angel Plane, and at the bottom, the Earth Plane where we exist (at the anus of the system!)

The famous American brain surgeon Eben Alexander[9],[10] has written two books relating to his experience arising from a serious attack of bacterial meningitis that left him brain dead in a coma for seven days. His surgeon colleagues asked the family if they could switch his life support off. Up to this time he was definitely not a religious person, and believed that at death a person's personality and all memories of this life are permanently extinguished, consistent with his scientific belief that the seat of a person's consciousness is only in their living brain. While seemingly brain dead he went to heaven, and now knows that at death the soul personality is not extinguished but continues to survive in an intensely vibrant reality that makes the earth plane experience completely boring in comparison! While in the spirit plane he met a sibling that he was totally unaware of. After his miraculous recovery and return to good health he saw a photograph of this dead sister for the first time, and only then realised that it was she that he had met on the spirit plane.

Need I say more? Of course, Eben Alexander could be lying. But I think not, because no one who was not absolutely 100% sure of what they were talking about would set themselves up for

---

9 Proof of Heaven by Ebn Alexander

10 The Map of Heaven by Ebn Alexander

public ridicule by describing their experience on the Oprah Winfrey television show and by writing books about it. To this day, no one can explain how or why Ebn Alexander contracted this severe disease. Similarly, no one can explain his miraculous recovery.

The fact that our highly developed science cannot **yet** prove the existence of the spirit plane is neither here nor there. One hundred years ago, colour television, and smart phones where you can talk to a friend on the other side of the earth, and see the live video of their face while you are talking to them, would have been derided as nonsense. What discoveries will science bring us in the next 10, 20 or even 50 years? Surely it will bring many things which are now only science fiction.

What's next? For myself, of course, I have no idea of what's next. I only know that I will accept it and make the best of it when it comes, including the moment when I fall off my perch at the end of this life and start on my next great adventure!

Printed in the United States
By Bookmasters